SOME AMERICAN PRIMITIVES

SOME AMERICAN PRIMITIVES: A Study of New England Faces and Folk Portraits

....

By CLARA ENDICOTT SEARS

....

KENNIKAT PRESS, INC./PORT WASHINGTON, N. Y.

PREFACE

This book is primarily for collectors, and for those who have a real interest in preserving what is now called the folk-art of America. These are not the grotesque examples that one comes across. I have a great shrinking from anything that departs from the normal. I leave such works for others to collect. My object is to gather together those portraits that are interesting and picturesque, and above all, that show signs of real artistic ability. Smothered talent has always seemed to me to be infinitely pathetic. It is therefore a joy to me to assemble in the collection I have made the portraits that indicate a talent that is capable of growing and developing into something that is beautiful, as has been the case with quite a number of those itinerant portrait painters who wandered from village to village and over the hillsides of New England in that 'yeasty' period when there existed every sort of talent, literary, artistic, and musical, as well as Transcendentalism, and the many 'isms of that day that bubbled up to the surface from 1700 and thereabouts to around 1860.

The collection has been gathered into a newly built picture gallery on the grounds of Fruitlands and the Wayside Museums, Incorporated, at Harvard, Massachusetts. It serves a double purpose: first, to show examples of the best work done by the old-time itinerant portrait painters of the nineteenth century, and also for the benefit of those who are now collecting, but who may not have had the opportunity to discover any like them. It is hoped that it will lead to the

[v]

unearthing of many of the names of artists as yet unacknow-
ledged, and their works. It will enable those who are searching for portraits of this kind to study various characteristics,
not only of those who are now well known, but also of the
humbler ones.

This is pioneer work.

It was the habit of artists great and small during that
period not to sign their paintings; therefore, the undoubted
talent of many of these men lies as yet unrecognized. If there
ever was a time when their names and their abilities can be
brought to the surface, it is now.

So many of these portraits were thrown away or burned up
or left to decay in the garrets of old houses that it will soon
be too late to collect those worthy of preservation unless it is
done at the present time. I am sending out the results of my
labors of years in hopes that they will prove to be of some
assistance and value.

The illustrations in this book are taken from the portraits
now in the picture gallery on the Museums grounds at Harvard, Massachusetts.

It has been a wonderful experience collecting them, and in
the book I have given an account of some of these experiences.
I have wandered through many towns and stopped at many
of the dear old houses in secluded New England villages, and
have found that the tide is turning and that now the old
people are clinging to these pictures of the past. They are
no longer being thrown away. They are being brought down
from the garrets and being hung on the best parlor walls of
quaint old farmhouses. In this collection, however, there are
some portraits of those belonging to a few of the more well-
to-do New England families. It has been my plan to begin
with real primitives and to show the gradations of talent that
led some of the itinerant portrait painters to develop into
artists of note, and in a few cases of international fame.

While the habit of not signing the paintings was very

prevalent, there were, of course, exceptions to the rule, as always happens, and I have been fortunate enough to find some of all grades that are signed, but they are very hard to find. They are apt to be signed on the back of the canvas with the name of the sitter and the date. If by chance they are signed on the front of the canvas, the signature will oftentimes be found tucked away in the most unexpected places, such as on the back of a letter or in the leaves of an open book, or almost anywhere you would not expect to find it. This encountering of the unexpected adds greatly to the interest of the collector.

CLARA ENDICOTT SEARS

HARVARD, MASSACHUSETTS, 1941

ACKNOWLEDGMENTS

The author desires to thank the following persons for the information they sent her:

Abbott, Mrs. Frederic B.
Alden, Miss Claire K.
Almy, Mr. Roger W.
Anderson, Mr. George P.
Anderson, Mrs. M. A.
Andrew, Mrs. J. A.
Armsby, Miss Lauribel
Atherton, Mr. Percy A.

Baker, Mr. Philip H.
Ball, Miss Elsie L.
Ball, Miss Lydia W.
Ballou, Mr. Charles E.
Barlow, Mrs. Arthur E.
Barteau, Mrs. E. L.
Bartholomew, Mrs. J. C.
Bartlett, Mr. A. Morandi
Bartlett, Miss Marion L.
Bates, Mr. Howard S.
Beers, Miss Mabel E.
Bennett, Mr. Chester A.
Bennett, Mr. W. W.
Bertram, Mrs. Ada S.
Bidwell, Miss Mildred T.
Blood, Miss Martha F.
Bolton, Mr. Charles K.
Bond, Miss Elizabeth L.

Brown, Mrs. William
Bushby, Mr. William

Canavan, Mrs. Emma S.
Carlson, Mrs. F. O. P.
Cavanagh, Mrs. Mary W.
Chace, Mrs. A. B.
Cheney, Mr. Walter C.
Clement, Mrs. Edith P.
Cobb, Mr. F. S.
Coffin, Mr. Edward F.
Cox, Miss Eleanor L.
Currier, Mrs. A. L.
Currier, Mr. T. Franklin
Cushing, Miss Jane D.
Cutler, Mr. A. Leon

Daniels, Miss Nellie H.
Dart, Mr. Frank S.
Day, Mrs. Rachel C.
Delaney, Miss Grace C.
de Langis, Mrs. R. L.
Dodd, Mr. George L.
Dods, Miss Agnes M.
Donnelly, Mrs. H. G.
Dutton, Mr. Charles H.
Dwinal, Mrs. Nellie S.

ACKNOWLEDGMENTS

Eastman, Miss Caroline C.
Eaton, Miss Alice E. S.
Emerson, Mr. William A.
Enos, Mrs. B. N.

Field, Mr. Edward
Fitzgerald, Miss Winnie
Flagg, Miss Abby E.
Flood, Mrs. Charles H.
French, Miss Isabel C.
Fry, Miss Katharine D.
Fuller, Mrs. Mary W.

Gardner, Mrs. R. F.
Gibson, Miss Florence B.
Gill, Mr. James M.
Gilpatric, Mrs. G. H.
Goddard, Miss Emma J.
Going, Miss Sarah
Green, Mrs. Elizabeth M. B.
Greene, Miss Sarah F.
Greene, Mrs. William M.
Gregory, Mr. H. S.

Hale, Mr. Richard W.
Hall, Mrs. Caroline D.
Hanscom, Miss Marion L.
Harney, Mr. E. C.
Haskell, Mr. Ira J.
Hathaway, Miss Margaret
Hayes, Mr. Harold J.
Hill, Miss Elisabeth S.
Hood, Mr. Chauncey W.
Hosmer, Miss Ella W.
Hosmer, Mrs. H. H.
Houde, Miss Shirley L.
Howard, Miss Bessie J.
Howe, Miss Edith M.

Huntington, Mr. Henry A.
Hurd, Mrs. C. I.

Jackson, Mrs. Charles H.
Jackson, Miss Rebena C.

Kennack, Mrs. Sarah C.
Kimball, Mrs. George E.
King, Mrs. James E.

Lawrence, Miss Alice A.
Lawrence, Mr. Carl A. P.
Leavitt, Mr. William H.
Ledward, Mrs. G. Arthur
Little, Mr. Harland
Long, Mrs. Charles L.

Malcolm, Mrs. E. P.
Mellen, Miss N. Theresa
Miller, Mrs. E. R.
Mills, Mrs. John T.
Mirick, Mrs. Abbie G.
Morse, Miss Constance
Munroe, Mrs. A. J.

Paradis, Miss Marie L.
Parker, Mrs. C. S.
Peirce, Miss Beulah M.
Perkins, Mrs. Charles B.
Phillips, Mrs. Eunice
Pinkham, Mrs. Gertrude E.
Pitt, Mrs. Thomas F.
Plummer, Mr. Walter F.
Pollard, Mr. Harold S.
Porter, Mrs. Ruth C.
Pray, Mr. Arthur E.
Prichard, Mrs. Sidney

Rand, Mrs. E. A.

[x]

ACKNOWLEDGMENTS

Reid, Miss M. Evelyn
Reid, Mrs. R. F., Jr.
Richards, Mr. Justin F.
Richardson, Mrs. C. F.
Richardson, Mr. J. Linwood

Safford, Miss Sue
Sanderson, Mr. George A.
Shugrue, Mr. M. F.
Smith, Miss Kate W.
Smith, Mrs. T. Gilman
Snow, Mrs. Morton
Spinney, Miss E. O.
Sprague, Miss Mary A.
Stammers, Mrs. Grace L.
Stolba, Mr. E. A.
Stone, Mr. C. F.
Stone, Miss Esther A.
Stone, Mrs. J. T.
Stupp, Miss Dorothy L.

Tainter, Mrs. A. B.
Taylor, Miss Elizabeth C.

Thurston, Miss Mary D.
Tilden, Mr. L. W.
Tolman, Miss Ethel G.
Trafton, Mrs. L. George

Van Wagner, Mr. Edward
Vaughan, Miss Dorothy M.
Vickery, Miss Helen E.
Vizard, Mrs. Emily S.

Walker, Mrs. Albert L.
Walker, Mr. M. Leon
Wellman, Mr. H. C.
Wheeler, Mrs. Amy C.
Wheeler, Mr. George
Wheeler, Miss Katharine A.
Wheelwright, Mr. John B.
White, Mr. William T.
Whitney, Mrs. A. L.
Whitney, Mr. William C.
Wilcox, Mr. J. Jay
Wilson, Mrs. Raymond H.
Wood, Mr. Harold S.

INDEX OF ARTISTS

INDEX OF ARTISTS

ILLUSTRATIONS

ILLUSTRATIONS

ILLUSTRATIONS

ILLUSTRATIONS

ILLUSTRATIONS

CHAPTER I

Time has woven a veil of romance around the memory of the old itinerant minstrels who followed the open road with their harps slung across their backs in mediaeval times in the lands across the sea, stopping at great stone castles, at scattered hamlets, at humble cottages, at village fairs, at royal tourneys, to mingle chords of music with the scene, or to sing before groups of gaily dressed lords and ladies of the court, or even before the king's throne, as the case might be.

Well, now, we too in our own country have had our itinerants following the open road, but they stopped at farmhouses with their overhanging elm trees, at villages, at fine old homesteads, even penetrating towns and cities, only they did not carry harps upon their backs, they carried a roll of canvases and brushes and a palette strapped to them to perpetuate the memory of faces of the living and sometimes of the dead with their crude spontaneous artistry.

They practised their art even in far-back Colonial days, but after the Revolution, when the sturdy inhabitants began to settle back and make permanent homes for themselves, and perhaps yearned a bit for the sense of background which they had always been conscious of in the old countries, the roving portrait painters were in great demand, and on the walls of homesteads, cottages, taverns, and wayside inns hung examples of their work. One interesting account of them mentions, 'The best bedroom was hung with family portraits, some of which were admirably executed.' (*History of American Painting*, by Samuel Isham.) Grandmother, with her lace cap and ample black silk or velvet dress, holding a book in her hand, was usually the first to be painted. Then came grandfather, with his high stock and waistcoat of satin or brocade. Then came the portraits of various children who had died in infancy, and the living children as well, and so on and so on until each generation was represented, and the homes became real homes, showing the history of the family and creating the background of which the inhabitants of the New Country had felt the lack.

We owe a debt of gratitude to these obscure wandering portrait painters, for how otherwise could we know what the people looked like who were forming the country in those days? And how otherwise could we have gained so clear an idea of what they wore, how they held themselves, what their esthetic interests were? For look at the many portraits of quaint old ladies that have been found holding a Bible in their hands, showing their strict adherence to the Sacred Book, and how many young women and even young men are portrayed holding a volume of poems, for those were days when romance was very much to the fore, and poets were held in high esteem.

The portraits told the story of the sitter. If he was a clergyman, he was sure to be shown holding a pen in his hand, and part of an unfinished sermon. If he followed the sea, there was apt to be the suggestion of a ship worked into the background. If he had attained the position of captain of a fine vessel sailing to and from the Orient, he was posed with chest thrust out, pompous in a blue coat with brass buttons, holding a compass in his hand, and so forth and so on.

From time immemorial there have been those possessed with a yearning to express themselves through the medium of art. Of such were the old-time itinerant portrait painters. Most of them began by doing odd jobs of painting on the farms, such as painting the buildings and so on. Others aspired to the painting of tavern signs, and coaches that drove

over the turnpikes with their relays of horses. These gave opportunity for creative work and allowed their imaginations
free play in regard to their love of color. Many a bright-hued
coach drawn by four trustworthy horses enlivened the country
roads as they carried the mail from one end of the state to the
other. Yellow was a very popular color and the doors were
often embellished with striking and intricate designs.

It so happened that most of the artists who emerged from
the ranks of itinerants into fame began by painting coaches.
When the first railroads were built, the train coaches were
quite fancy, which provided another outlet for the inventive
talents of the wandering artists until they could venture forth
on the open road in quest of subjects for portraits, which was
the special goal towards which one and all were struggling.
Their ways of procedure were about the same, although some
were more pertinacious than others. As they went along they
would stop at some comfortable-looking farmhouse with an
air of well-being about it.

Here is the way one of the good artists, named William
Thompson, did, when he stopped at the old Aaron Whitney
homestead in Harvard, Massachusetts, about one hundred
years ago. His method of stirring up business for himself was
very effective, and, more than that, it brought results. Evidently old Aaron Whitney thought him convincing, for he
took him into his house for one whole winter, and for his
board and lodging Thompson painted eight portraits of the
Whitney family, which showed that he was an enterprising
and industrious artist, to say the least. Three of these portraits hang on the walls of the home of his great-granddaugh-
ter. The others are distributed among the rest of the
family.

The old Whitney homestead was situated about two miles
from the centre of Harvard village, where it is generally be-
lieved that Thompson painted other portraits than those already mentioned. If so, one can picture him travelling over

the narrow roads, carrying his canvases on his back, and reaching home at sundown in time for supper and a long chat with his host by the kitchen fire as they smoked their comforting pipes through the long winter evenings.

Fortunately, one of the Whitney portraits is signed. It is the one he painted of the head of the family, to whom he owed this winter of contentment. This brings him out of a practically forgotten past into the history of the folk-art of New England as a reality and not a myth. It was dated 1841.

Where he came from or where he went to after leaving Harvard is still a mystery, but one of the fascinating points of searching for clues of some of these old itinerant portrait painters and saving them from oblivion is the fact that at almost any turn of the road one may come across something, or hear something, or see something that leads to discovery. A very old person in one of the towns may furnish a clue to follow, or one may come across another of his portraits, perhaps, which may reveal much. I can speak feelingly on the subject, for I was determined to find out something, however small it might be, about this William Thompson, as he had painted so many portraits in Harvard, Massachusetts; so one day I went to the American Antiquarian Society in Worcester, and there they brought out some of the old newspapers of his time. With dogged perseverance I scanned the papers eagerly one by one, when suddenly I came upon the following advertisement:

William Thompson — Portrait Painting
Has taken a room opposite the
Central Bank for a few days.

The public is invited to call and see
specimens. September 13, 1837.

This shows that before he went to Harvard he was painting portraits in near-by towns, so one may come across them at any time, unless the descendants of the original owners have sold them or destroyed them, or put them with their faces to the wall in the attic, and forgotten them. But the eight portraits of the Whitney family remain as witnesses of his winter in the old town of Harvard and the work he did there.

Strange to say, though Thompson is a name to be found almost as easily as Smith in ordinary life, when it comes to the arts it is rather unusual. There is a portrait in the picture gallery at Fruitlands and the Wayside Museums, Incorporated, at Harvard, Massachusetts, which is signed by that name. It is a portrait of Mr. Bird, and the signature reads, 'Mr. Thompson, Artist, 1839, Brookfield, Mass.' This portrait (page 13) is more important in size and execution than the portraits of the Whitney family by William Thompson, and is of an earlier date. The sitter was evidently a man of importance in a small town. He is a bit ungainly in figure, but for all that he has dignity of bearing, and his black hair, ruddy face, and shrewd, intelligent brown eyes hold one's attention. The coloring of the picture is deep and rich in tone. His coat and trousers are black, and well set off by a dark golden-brown waistcoat. Around his throat is a royal blue silk choker. In his hand he holds a book of a bright vermilion color. The tint is repeated in the seals on the letters lying on a table next to his elbow. The chair he sits in is of mahogany. The inevitable draped curtain behind him is reddish-brown, melting into a dull red as it touches the other side of the canvas. Taken as a whole the portrait is very characteristic of the type of man that it portrays. It is very well painted, attracts one's attention, and is pleasing to the eye. One amusing point in it is the fact of the artist's signing his name on one of the letters on the table. He has put 'paid' in one corner, which has a thrifty little look to it, and one feels sure it was done at the instigation of the sitter, Mr. Bird, who may have thought it was unwise to leave anything at loose ends.

Two fine portraits of which the little town of Harvard,

Massachusetts, can be proud were painted and signed by an artist named L. Pollard. They were portraits (pages 14 and 15) of a very well-known inhabitant, John Farwell, with his faithful dog 'Hero,' and of his wife, Emeline (Whipple) Farwell. These have been presented by their granddaughter to the collection of the work of the old-time itinerant portrait painters opened to the public last summer in the new picture gallery at Fruitlands and the Wayside Museums, Incorporated, at Harvard, Massachusetts, of which the author of this book is the founder. They are extremely well painted, and were highly praised by the critics who visited the collection. The background of both portraits is smoke-color. John Farwell is young and good-looking with dark brown hair. He wears a black coat, a broad black satin tie, and white vest, all cut in the old-fashioned way. The chair he sits in is red, and at his knees sits his dog, a big black Newfoundland with searching eyes. His wife in the companion portrait has pretty light brown hair, pink cheeks, and blue eyes. Her black silk dress has puffed sleeves, and over her shoulders is a muslin scarf. She is rather delicate-looking and is the pure New England type. These portraits were painted in 1845 according to the signature.

Now, the Pollard family in Harvard dates back to very early days, and the lovely old house on the Common is still occupied by one of that name. In that family was a man by the name of Luke Pollard, and since the portrait was painted in Harvard, it would seem that he must have been an artist and painted those portraits, especially as he was a neighbor of Mr. John Farwell's in the old days. There are even one or two in the town who, as children, played in the Pollard barn, and they remember having seen a dozen or more oil paintings lying around in the hay. They used to wonder who painted them. The paintings were old and beaten from exposure and neglect, and young as the children were, it seemed strange to them that they should be left to decay in an old barn like that one. Sometime later the paintings disappeared, and the neighbors could never find out what became of them. This seems to indicate a possibility, and even a probability, that the L. Pollard of the signature might well be the Luke Pollard of the old Pollard homestead, and that these oil paintings seen by the children might be some of his work. That seems to have been the general impression. At the same time, these Farwell portraits have a great deal of merit, and show a knowledge and experience which adds to the mystery.

I received a letter from a stranger telling me that the Concord Historical Society was exhibiting a portrait listed as 'Luke Pollard and Cummins Davis,' and claimed it was painted by Luke Pollard himself. I hurriedly went in search of it, and, to my chagrin, I found it had been removed the day before, so I was too late. But I made very careful inquiries about it, and was told it was a self-portrait of Luke Pollard with his friend, Cummins Davis, painted on the same canvas, and the owner was Mr. Harold S. Davis of Harvard, Massachusetts. It was during a telephone conversation with Mr. Davis on the subject that he said he had never heard of his having been an artist. But then he may never have heard of the pictures rotting away in the old barn, and as he lives in New York, many of these traditions may have escaped him. No one knows what to think about it. The American Antiquarian Society of Worcester, Massachusetts, is on the watch for a solution of the mystery, as well as others who are interested, especially myself.

In the meantime, a Luke Pollard has been found among the annals of Lancaster, Massachusetts, and another by that name has been found, I believe, in Bolton, Massachusetts, if I am not mistaken. But the L. Pollard who painted the portraits was of an earlier date. Here is a mystery yet to be solved; suffice it to say, the portraits are very well painted, and are very charming.

[7]

Anyone who was striving to be recognized as an artist in those days had to pass through the itinerant stage until he had become well known and sought after. There was no other way of bringing himself before the public. It meant persistent and arduous work to reach that point. Advertising was rarely resorted to on account of the expense, and most of these men were without funds to draw from, the young ones especially. Transportation was a big question to consider, and that cost money too. The stage-coaches ran on certain days only. In the country districts a newspaper would drift into a village once a week, but not oftener. For a young man with ambition the only way to do was to tie his belongings in a bandana handkerchief and sling it over his shoulder with his canvases and palette and brushes and make for the open road, taking whatever chances came his way to show his art. It was a long road in most cases.

The public called these adventurous wanderers 'limners,' and taken as a whole the profession was looked upon as of little importance and was classed by some in the category of scissors-grinders, or peddlers, and the like. They all had to fight against this handicap, and it took determination and ambition to overcome it. Those who did, and who forged their way up to the front ranks of the art world, and whose names are written on the pages of the history of their times, are to be honored for the struggles they had to face and conquer.

As one and all started from the same point of having had no instruction in the art of portrait painting, it soon became evident that some far outran others from sheer latent talent. These were divided into two classes, those who worked primarily for the sake of building up a competency on which to live and raise their families, and so made use of their artistic gifts of execution and imagination continually to further that cause, and those who, enamored of Art for its own sake, sought every means that came their way to mount higher and higher in the scale. These last belonged to the class that emerged from the itinerant limitations and had been so fortunate as to be able to put aside money enough to become pupils of some outstanding artist in the bigger world of Art, and from there on to forge their way up into the ranks of eminent portrait painters such as Chester Harding, Francis Alexander, James Frothingham, and others of whom our country is proud.

From out of the former class of those who made the business end the important factor came many of the quaint tricks of the trade of which one hears so much. It was not every housewife who could produce a silk or velvet dress to be painted in, so the versatile artists put in a stock of costumes for the benefit of their patrons which they could choose from. One finds the same dress figuring in a number of portraits in one locality, with small changes made, such as adding a lace fichu here and a ribbon bow there, or even transforming a dress from high-neck to low-neck according to the wishes of a sitter. The sleeves and the body of the dress usually remained unchanged, as in the case of the 'Wood girls' from Townsend, Massachusetts (one of whom became Mrs. Pierce), whose portraits are in the picture gallery of the Wayside Museums at Harvard, Massachusetts. The illustrations on pages 16 and 18 will give a sample of this. The dress in this case is black velvet. The only change made was around the neck. As no velvet dress could ever have come out of the old Wood farm on Townsend Hill, it is safe to infer that the artist, whoever he was, belonged to this class. The pictures are very quaint and were very evidently good likenesses, and the artist knew how to convey their salient characteristics. The sister with the smooth hair one feels was sensitive and rather apprehensive, and probably died of consumption as so many did in those days, for there is a red flush on her cheekbones which denotes it. The other sister gives one the impression of being a young woman who had rather a nervous, difficult disposition and was addicted to patent medicines bought at the country store, for her nose is rather red. In those days these itinerant artists did not flatter their sitters; they painted just what they saw.

The portrait (page 17) of Mr. Pierce, husband of the lady who probably died of consumption, shows an exceedingly good-looking young man with a perfectly fitted black velvet coat, high at the back of the neck, and a waistcoat of yellow satin which apparently was a little too snug for him, for it seems to button with some difficulty down by the waistline, and shows a glimpse of white shirt from underneath. The black stock wound around his neck with two small points of white collar showing above it is very becoming to him. He has that fatal lock of hair falling over his forehead, and he wears sideburns. The portrait was painted about 1843, but the artist is unknown.

Quite a number of the itinerant portrait painters had a room on the top floor of buildings on Tremont Street in Boston. There they kept their extra stores of materials for their work, and it was no uncommon sight to see them emerge from there in the early morning with canvases on their backs and bundles of paint brushes and paints under their arms ready to start forth to capture sitters, sometimes not returning for weeks at a time. In those days it was a recognized trade, and in some cases a profitable one. It made an appeal to a young man for the variety of experiences it brought him. Sometimes romance crept in to give an added zest to his work. The ground they covered and the variety of persons they came in contact with made them a very entertaining addition to the simple households they entered in the country districts, and as a rule they fared pretty well.

The prices they received for their work varied considerably. Some charged from four to five or seven dollars for painting a portrait. Others went as high as twelve, and worked their way up to fifteen if they were in demand. Even the renowned Francis Alexander in his itinerant days got only five dollars for the full-length portrait of a child. Then as he worked his way up he raised his price to fifteen dollars, again to twenty-five, then to forty and fifty, and finally to seventy-five dollars. When he had acquired his great reputation, he could demand the high price compatible with the position he held as an artist. With James Frothingham it was much the same way. Chester Harding, of course, could ask what he pleased, owing in a large measure to the unprecedented success of the work he did in England, where the aristocracy and the members of the court flocked to his studio while he was there. These three men stand out pre-eminently against a background of wandering artists, having begun their careers as one of that group, but through their own talents and tenacious perseverance finally emerged from it and climbed to the top of their profession and were acknowledged by the world of Art.

Then came the lesser lights who also emerged from the itinerant class, like Ethan Allen Greenwood (who painted some beautiful portraits), Albert Gallatin Hoit, Joseph Greenleaf Cole, and others, and after them a long line of wandering artists, many of whom showed great talent in the work they did, but whose names faded into the twilight zone after they died. They are now being unearthed by collectors and brought into the light again. Then there were those whose work never moved out of the class of what is known as 'primitives.' Some of these, too, had their own points of excellence, and at the present time are being sought after and tabulated as examples of the folk-art of American painting.

It seems to have been the habit for artists not to sign their pictures. A very unfortunate habit it was, and one which has cast an impenetrable veil of mystery over work that should receive acknowledgment. Even the accepted leaders did not do so as a rule. The great Copley himself was one of the outstanding offenders, as was also Gilbert Stuart, the most brilliant planet of all in our sky of portrait painting. Artists of that calibre probably took it for granted that their style of painting spoke for itself and needed no signature. But the lesser lights followed suit, and though they broke through their rule at times, the signed pictures are few and far between. Sometimes when they were painting the portraits of a husband and wife they would put their signature on one of them, leaving the other unsigned. They seemed to 'take no thought of the morrow' in regard to their work, and never realized that at some future time these portraits might become separated, and thus cause confusion. Sometimes the sitters required a signature, but in most cases they gave it no thought, the portrait itself being the important factor.

Now, there came a time when the old folks who had cherished their portraits with such fondness were no longer there to take care of them, and the younger generations lost interest in them. They did not care to be surrounded with portraits of those who had gone. It depressed them. So the latter were dethroned from their positions of importance on the walls and were ignominiously consigned to the garret, where the dust of years accumulated on them and they were forgotten, except when a man would come around looking for old frames; then their tarnished glory would be stripped from them and they became not much more than old junk in the eyes of the descendants, and were left to the rats and the mice and threatened oblivion.

But fortunately, there were some of a more sensitive type who kept them still hanging in the best parlor, opened for family occasions, and to these also we owe a debt of gratitude; for the time has come when the public is anxious to keep alive the old traditions and to preserve those things which were valued in former days and which reopen vistas of the past. Then, too, modern art is adopting some of the methods and spontaneous visualizing of the old-time itinerant portrait painters. To prove this, a few excerpts are taken from

PORTRAIT OF SAMUEL BIRD OF BROOKFIELD, MASSACHUSETTS
Painted by 'Mr. Thompson' in 1839.
(Description, page 5)

PORTRAIT OF JOHN FARWELL AND HIS FAITHFUL DOG 'HERO,'
HARVARD, MASSACHUSETTS
Painted by Luke Pollard about 1845.
(Description, page 6)

PORTRAIT OF EMELINE WHIPPLE FARWELL, HARVARD,
MASSACHUSETTS
Painted by Luke Pollard about 1845.
(Description, page 6)

[15]

PORTRAIT OF MRS. PIERCE OF TOWNSEND, MASSACHUSETTS
Artist unknown. Painted about 1843.
(Description, page 9)

PORTRAIT OF MR. PIERCE OF TOWNSEND, MASSACHUSETTS
Artist unknown. Painted about 1843.
(Description, page 10)

[17]

PORTRAIT OF MISS WOOD OF TOWNSEND, MASSACHUSETTS
Artist unknown. Painted about 1843.
(Description, pages 9, 10)

PORTRAIT OF A YOUNG MAN OF MIDDLESEX COUNTY,
MASSACHUSETTS
Artist unknown. Painted about 1836.
(Description, pages 189, 190)

[19]

PORTRAIT OF A YOUNG MAN FROM NEW BEDFORD,
MASSACHUSETTS

*Painted by William Matthew Prior in 1844 (after he had changed to his
Fall River-Sturbridge style of painting).*

(Description, page 42)

PORTRAIT OF MRS. CHASE OF SOUTH DENNIS, MASSACHUSETTS

Painted by William Matthew Prior in 1844 (after he had changed to his
Fall River-Sturbridge style of painting).
(Description, page 43)

[21]

PORTRAIT OF H. B. WEBB, ESQ., OF BATH, MAINE
(SHIPBUILDER)
Painted by William Matthew Prior in 1831.
(Description, page 43)

[22]

PORTRAIT OF A YOUNG MATRON OF STURBRIDGE, MASSACHUSETTS
Painted after the Fall River-Sturbridge School of Painting. Artist unknown.
(Description, pages 44, 45)

[23]

PORTRAIT OF A GENTLEMAN OF STURBRIDGE, MASSACHUSETTS
(HUSBAND OF THE YOUNG MATRON)
Painted after the Fall River-Sturbridge School of Painting. Artist unknown.
(Description, page 45)

[24]

PORTRAIT OF A YOUNG WOMAN OF STURBRIDGE, MASSACHUSETTS
Painted after the Fall River-Sturbridge School of Painting. Artist unknown.
(Description, pages 46, 47)

[25]

PORTRAIT OF A GENTLEMAN OF STURBRIDGE, MASSACHUSETTS
(HUSBAND OF THE YOUNG WOMAN)
Painted after the Fall River-Sturbridge School of Painting. Artist unknown.
(Description, page 47)

[26]

PORTRAITS OF JOHN AND MARY WILLIAMS OF PEPPERELL, MASSACHUSETTS

Artist unknown.

(Description, pages 47–49)

PORTRAIT OF A WOMAN
Painted by G. Alden about 1844. (A good example of a primitive.)
(Description, page 49)

published opinions of critics connected with some of our best museums where exhibitions of early American portraits have been held. They are as follows:

The Museum of Newark, New Jersey, held an Exhibition of the Nineteenth Century Folk-Artists, in 1930 and 1931, and the following estimate was incorporated into the Catalogue:

> The Newark Museum is showing these paintings, not because they are quaint or curious, but because they are interesting documents in the history of American Folk-Art, and have a genuine esthetic feeling. It generally happens in the development of an art that these isolated artists, who had to struggle to realize their forms of expression, have unconsciously put more freshness and vigor into their work than those who were able to work with ease. The sincere untutored painter must so concentrate on his problems that affectation is out of the question, and his honest intensity is reflected in his work. Thus, some of these primitive pictures affect one like a breath of fresh air after viewing the more skilled products of Academic Schools. Their spirit, at once serious and gay, more than compensates for the artist's lack of technical knowledge.
>
> It is easy to understand why modern painters are enthusiastic about them, for, in spite of the sophistication of this age, painters are trying to approach their subject with a similar attitude.... This scattered unsophisticated work, as a whole, is the nearest thing we have to really native art. The zest of these (itinerant) painters for their subject, their highly individual expression, and their natural esthetic sense make of their work a refreshing contribution to the history of American painting.... Men like these were artists by nature — the peculiar charm of their work results sometimes from what would be technical inadequacies from the Academic point of view. But they were not simply artists who lack adequate training. The work of the best of them has a directness, a unity, and a power which one does not always find in the work of standard masters. (Newark Museum Catalogue.)

The European influence is at the heart of the native American development. Certain influences, Dutch or English, mainly, are definitely recognizable. Most of these artists had seen paintings of one kind or another, or had seen engravings in books. It is evident that they tried to approximate effects by academic artists. (Holger Cahill, in 'American Primitives,' Newark Museum Catalogue.)

The following is an excerpt from the Catalogue of 'An Exhibition of American Folk-Painting,' held in October, 1930, by the Harvard Society of Contemporary Art, in Cambridge, Massachusetts:

> The chief charm of folk-painting lies in the deviation from Academic models, the exaggeration of certain features bound to impress the provincial — small details seized upon by virtue of familiarity and rendered with particular absorption... a purity of linear handling, a deep psychological insight in portraiture, a freshness of color combined with the use of original media, and an honesty that is as gracious as it is disarming.... More often than not, these painters created distinguished work. (From Catalogue of the Exhibition of American Folk-Painting.)

This growing appreciation of the work of these early artists makes it doubly worth while to collect and safeguard whatever specimens we can find of it, and to learn what we can of the men themselves, for their type has gone and probably will never return. They belonged to the so-called 'good old times.'

CHAPTER II

Perhaps some of the most sought-after portraits by the old-time itinerant portrait painters today are those by William M. Prior. It may be because he was especially daring in his methods, sometimes joining the essentially primitive artists, sometimes painting in a more serious mood after the authorized style. He was not biased in any way by public opinion. He followed his mood. The result was that his work was very spontaneous, and it seemed to be appreciated by the public even in those days and by all the seaport towns on the coast to begin with, and later on by broader fields. He was essentially a product of New England.

Prior was born in Bath, Maine, in 1806, and was the son of a Duxbury shipbuilder and was exceedingly proud of the stock from which he came.

It was my good fortune to be taken to see an old gentleman just approaching the age of ninety, one day two years ago, by a friend of his family. This old gentleman was Mr. Matthew Prior, son of the old itinerant artist, William Matthew Prior.

I shall always remember that visit. It was in the late afternoon when the days were growing short. In response to the tinkle of the front doorbell, a sweet little lady of the old school ushered us into the room where the old gentleman was sitting. The little lady was his niece by marriage, and she whispered to him that two ladies had come to see him. His chair was drawn close to the window so as to get all of the now fading light, and he was hard at work painting on glass, which was one of the avenues of art frequently used by his father when old age came upon him. He was so absorbed in his work that it took several minutes before he realized that there was a stranger in the room. When he turned towards me, I hastily explained the reason of my visit. I told him I was planning to write about the itinerant portrait painters of the early nineteenth century, and was anxious to learn from him something about his father. He at once put down his paint brush, and leaned back in his chair with a smile of pleasure on his face. He did not speak for a few minutes.

I glanced about the room. It seemed to me full of shadows. The light from the embers from the old Franklin stove was the one gleam of warmth, except for the luminous sunset sky that shone through the windows. I noticed on the wall a portrait of a young man with a palette and brush in his hand. My friend whispered to me that it was the self-portrait of William M. Prior which was painted in 1830. Then she pointed to another portrait on the wall and whispered that it was that of his brother. There was still another of a small boy holding a whip, painted on cardboard, which she told me was the portrait of a son of the artist. I looked at them with astonishment, for they were not painted in the style that I associated with Prior's work.

I was so taken up with looking at them and the details around me that I was almost startled when the old gentleman said: 'My father — yes — my father was thought a great deal of. He used to start out early in the morning and always found plenty of work to do. It seems he was an independent young man, full of ambition, and he worked his way up in the scales so fast that in his early twenties he painted a portrait of A. Hammett, Esq. It was exhibited at the Boston Athenaeum in 1831. When he was a small boy he painted the portrait of a neighbor on the barn door, which created quite an excitement in the village. Yes, he heard considerable about it. Young as he was, he made up his mind then and there to become an artist, and when he was old enough he took up the trade of the itinerant portrait painter, walking along the dusty roads with a pack on his back.'

It was easy to see that telling about his father gave the old man supreme enjoyment. 'Did he marry early?' I asked. 'Well,' he answered, 'about the time most young men marry, and with his painting he had accumulated enough money with which to buy a piece of land on Trenton Street in East Boston; number 36 was the number of the house he built upon it. It was a plain enough house, but it suited him. My father had all sorts of notions. He had a beehive under the roof, for one thing, and those bees went all over the city to get honey, even as far as the Public Garden in the springtime. But they always came back to the hive, and they supplied enough honey for the use of him and his family. The house he named the "Painting Garret." Whenever he signed his name on a portrait at the back of the canvas you will find 36 Trenton Street, East Boston, also on it as a rule.'

There was another pause, and we waited several minutes before he spoke again. 'Father was always an itinerant portrait painter, but now he acquired a horse and wagon, and accompanied by his wife he would start out with the back of the wagon full of canvases, and in this way he journeyed far afield throughout this state and other states as well, where, to this day, you may run across his paintings. When his two children grew out of babyhood, he carried them along with him, which made quite a family party, so it must have been quite a circumstance to put them all up for the purpose of getting a portrait painted. It was the habit of the day to give these artists food and lodging, which was included in the price of the portrait.'

I remarked on the excellence of the portrait William M. Prior painted of himself. He was a romantic-looking young man with a black coat and broad velvet collar. A white stock was wrapped around his throat. His features were well formed, and there was a thoughtful look in his face. 'Yes,' said my host, 'some say it was the best picture he had ever painted and a good likeness.'

Then I saw that the old man was getting a little bit tired, and was glancing longingly at the work he had been doing when we came in, so I asked him about it. He told me that his father often painted portraits on glass, especially the portraits of noted characters such as George Washington and Martha Washington, Lincoln, Grant, Theodore Parker, and the like, and framed them in narrow gilt frames and sold them. People seemed to like them, and were willing to pay several dollars for them. 'He taught me how to do it, and, as you can see, I have quite a stack of them here.'

I felt anxious not to outstay my welcome, so I got up and bade him good-bye, remarking that I should be very glad if he would let me come to see him again, and he said I might. As I reached the door, I looked back and saw the old gentleman eagerly bending over his work again with his paint brush poised in one hand and his palette in the other, and even in the fading light he was putting some finishing touches to a picture of a ship in full sail.

It appears that from 1847 to 1852 Prior had a room at 18 Tremont Street, where he kept his painting supplies. His first wife, Rosamond Hamblen by name, died in Boston in 1849, leaving four children, two girls and two boys. Prior was too busy a man to carry on a family without a woman to look after things, so he took to himself another wife a year later. She was Hannah Frances Walworth, of Andover, and was only twenty years old at the time of her marriage. He took her to his house, 36 Trenton Street, East Boston. If it had been a palace he could not have been prouder of it. From the upper story he could look out to Boston Harbor and see the ships coming and going. It spelled romance to him. He came of people who went 'down to the sea in ships,' and to all those thus born the sea means something that nothing else means. So it was with him.

Now, in my search for details regarding the life of William M. Prior, I had another very illuminating experience. I had advertised in a local paper that covers the towns surrounding Harvard, Massachusetts, asking if anyone had any information to give me regarding the old-time itinerant portrait painters of the early nineteenth century, of which there had been a great many throughout the state. Almost immediately I received a letter from a granddaughter of the artist Prior. She was living near the outskirts of Groton, about six miles from my home in Harvard, Massachusetts. Needless to say, I lost no time in following the directions she gave me to find the house she was living in.

I found her in a tiny cottage by the roadside. It was evidently very old. I approached the door and knocked. An old lady, somewhat bent, with a sensitive, refined face, opened it, and after greeting me very gently and sweetly ushered me into a room strewn with oil paintings, some very old and some half-finished. One especially I noticed that was on an easel that was in the process of being painted. Beside it lay a palette and a bunch of brushes. 'Still another Prior at work painting!' I said to myself with astonishment.

Mrs. Malcolm — that was her name, Edith Prior Malcolm — asked me to be seated, and then she would tell me what she remembered about her grandfather. I did so, placing a notebook and pencil in my lap, ready to jot down all the information I could gather.

She said she was glad to tell me about her grandfather because she had just passed her eightieth birthday, and she wanted someone besides herself to know about him as a man, apart from the artist. Her first recollection of him revealed a tender heart. Not but what he was strict when he wanted to be, for he would never allow his grandchildren to come to the room which he had put aside for himself, and in which

he finished the portraits he had on hand which he had commenced during his itinerant wanderings, but had not had
sufficient time to complete at the sittings. The result was
that they looked upon it as a room of mystery, full of fairy
tales and what not. But here is a specimen of his kind heart.

His second daughter was named Balona. She was handsome
but somewhat flighty in her ways. On one occasion his eldest
daughter, Mrs. Gilbert Stuart Prior (Mrs. Malcolm's mother),
who lived in a little house near her father's, was called away
to a meeting or something of the sort, and she asked her
sister, always known as 'Aunt Balona,' to stay with the
children while she was gone, and warned her to be sure not
to leave them for a moment. Aunt Balona said, 'Oh, all
right,' and it was left that way. But after what seemed like
a very short time the young woman began to stretch and
yawn and to get up and look out of the door. Apparently it
was too much for her. Suddenly, putting on her hat, she left
the house, leaving these small youngsters all alone. They
ran to the window thinking she would come back, but she
did not come. They began to be frightened, and went back
into the room and sat on the floor together.

Pretty soon they saw their grandfather's face pressed against
the window-pane. He was trying to peer into the room where
they were. The children hailed him with joy, and he came
quickly into the house.

'Are you all alone? Where's your Aunt Balona?' he asked.

'She's gone,' they answered.

'And left you all alone?'

'Yes,' they said.

He made no remark, but took off his hat and sat down. It
was one of his busy days. He was right in the midst of putting
finishing touches to one of his portraits that he had expected
to deliver shortly. But while doing so he remembered that
his oldest daughter had said she was going off for some hours
and had asked their Aunt Balona to look after the children

while she was gone. He became troubled. Finally he put on his hat and hurried over to his daughter's house near-by to see if all was well. He had half-expected what he found. Time went on and the afternoon was drawing to a close, but still he sat on, talking to the children and amusing them as best he could until his daughter's return, when he delivered them into her hands safe and sound. It had practically broken up his whole working day, but he did it without a murmur. He was very fond of his family.

Mrs. Malcolm said she always liked to remember that little episode, because her grandfather was rather an eccentric man, and could be very cross when he wanted to be, but this showed that at heart he was all right.

Like all followers of the arts, he was very temperamental and emotional, and when in 1840 and 1843 William Miller went about the countryside warning people that the end of the world was near at hand, Prior was very much stirred and impressed by him and his prophecy. He went to all the meetings that were held near Boston and became what you might call a follower. He admired Miller enormously, and finding that the latter had a daughter named Balona he gave his second daughter that name, and also inserted the name of Miller into the names of the others with the exception of his second son, who was named after another of his 'heroes,' Gilbert Stuart.

Just before the appointed year when the dissolution of the world was to take place, Miller held many meetings in and around Boston and an excitement bordering on hysteria was seizing hold of the public. Prior went to all the meetings, but he became so excited and shouted so loud, insisting upon prophesying on his own hook, describing what was going to take place with such a vivid imagination, that the audience rebelled, and the family decided to send Aunt Balona with him in the future. When he got wrought up into more or less of a frenzy, she would drag him out of the hall still shouting and prophesying, but at least the audience was free of him and could listen to William Miller, who was explaining his reasons for having come to believe that the time had arrived for people to prepare for the great event.

After that Prior joined the Spiritualists and became an enthusiastic convert. He had several children by his second wife, who died young. He claimed he could follow them into the Spirit World and see every detail of their faces so clearly that he could paint their portraits, which he proceeded to do. This made a great impression on many whose children had died, and he reaped a harvest from this branch of his work.

He had curious views about his son. He did not want him to choose his profession or to do work of any kind, and the young man ran away from home three times to secure a job in a machine shop, for he had a great leaning towards mechanics. His father promptly went after him and told him 'he would rather he would race the streets than have his children servants to anyone.' So his son did 'race the streets' more often than not, and became more or less of a ne'er-do-weel. The secret reason that made Prior take such a stand with him was because, like many other fathers, he wanted him to follow in his own footsteps. With Gilbert Stuart Prior for a name he thought he might go far. The results were pretty disastrous. However, it is only fair to mention here that, though the young man led a somewhat disorganized life, he did join the army at the time of the Civil War, so at least he served his country in its hour of need. We must also be fair to Aunt Balona and record the fact that once, when her brother was put in jail for some misdemeanor, she paid her little nest-egg of two hundred dollars to get him out, which was greatly to her credit.

But to go back to William M. Prior's work. He was fussy about his paints and always ground them himself, but he was not so fussy about his canvases. If one of these were lacking, he would use almost anything that came handy. He painted a portrait of Andrew Jackson in one sitting on a piece of bed-ticking. Sometimes he used cardboard, and with good results too.

'He was evidently a great worker,' I ventured, wishing to hear more.

Mrs. Malcolm nodded her head. 'When I visited the library at Bowdoin College,' she said, 'I saw a book there written by my grandfather, named *The King's Venture.*

'He must have been a really inveterate worker, but he loved work. I have heard my mother say that sometimes he would have as many as two hundred portraits piled up in his paint-ing garret waiting to have the finishing touches put on them.'

I asked her to name some of the prominent men he had painted, and she replied: 'Well, once when Charles Dickens was in Boston he painted a portrait of him, and painted it at the Revere House, where the author was staying. There were others, but I have forgotten them for the moment. But he did a number on glass, I know. He had a great longing to copy the portrait of George Washington by Gilbert Stuart that hangs in the Boston Athenaeum. After three years he received permission to do this, much to his great joy, for he was an enthusiast about Stuart's work.'

'Did he ever try painting landscapes?' I asked.

'Yes, he did paint some,' she said, and she took from out of the closet a moonlight scene in oils, on the back of which was Prior's stamp with his signature; also the 'Painting Garret, 36 Trenton Street, East Boston, Mass.' Mrs. Malcolm then told me that her grandfather had often said that he had never seen a picture which satisfactorily gave the glow of moonlight, so he tried painting one himself, and this was the one. He called it 'Moonlight.' He certainly got the glow of the moonlight in the picture. It was quite striking in a small way, and had the charm of many of the old landscapes painted at that period. I am glad now that I secured it for

[39]

my collection. It was an auspicious day for me when I went into that little cottage to see Mrs. Malcolm. She certainly gave me a great deal of information. She was so earnest about it, and so interested, that the hours I spent there (for I went more than once) were especially pleasant ones to look back upon.

In regard to the change in Prior's style of painting, it is difficult to know what occasioned it, as to whether it was a forerunner of the modern style, which is very similar, or whether it was expediency, as he had so many portraits to paint and it took less time. Mrs. Malcolm was under the impression that the change took place the year that the Fall River Mills were closed. Prior happened to be there at the time and was doing a great deal of work there and at New Bedford, and all the portraits that he painted at that period and from then on differed so completely from what he had done before that it seems that there must have been some fundamental change in his views on painting. One of the reasons that so many of the young people nowadays and the young artists admire Prior's work is because he evidently saw something in his art that they now see in their own. It is a complete change of values. If you go to any of the exhibitions of Picasso's portraits or of others of his school, you will find one or two there that could easily have been painted by Prior.

I received a letter from a lady in New Bedford in answer to an advertisement I had put in one of the newspapers asking for information in regard to the itinerant portrait painters, and she says:

'My grandmother and her sister conducted a young ladies' seminary in Newport, Rhode Island, until 1826 or 1827, when she married. They were frequent visitors to Newport, where they met one Pryor or Prior, an artist, in 1848, who was painting portraits of the Wilbur family and other Newport people. He was invited to New Bedford to paint the children of grandfather and grandmother, of which there were nine. He came in 1849 and painted seven of the children (the older ones being employed in the Newport Library), ranging from two to seventeen years. Prior was a guest in the home for many weeks, and I have heard members of the family say that his method was to draw very sketchy outlines of his subject and paint them while the children were in school. The paintings look more like the old-fashioned canvas dolls with the painted faces with almost no expression. Still they are very cute and everyone admires them. We have the one of my father who was sixteen when done and my aunt who was about two. My father had a Dutch haircut, very loose clothing and a small book in his hands, presumably a Bible, as they were very religious people. My aunt wore a little dress off the shoulders, gathered at the waistline, and a string of coral beads, and holds a tiny toy rabbit in her hands, and her hair is combed straight back. This is about all I can tell you about the subject.

'Sincerely hoping this slight information may prove of some help to you, I remain,

'Yours very truly,

'(Signed) ——'

It is this style of portrait now that one associates with Prior, and if the modern artists are seeing things along that same line and admiring them, it would seem that Prior had had more or less of the same vision that they have when he changed his method of painting so radically. His work is usually listed among the 'primitives.' It is that same quality of primitiveness in the work of Picasso and the other artists of his style of painting that links them up with Prior, the old itinerant portrait painter.

After hearing these details about him and his family, I was doubly anxious to procure specimens of his work, and it was not long after that that I came across two portraits signed by him, one of a young man from New Bedford, painted in 1844, and the other of an old lady with spectacles on, a Mrs. Chase of Dennis, Massachusetts. I felt somehow as though they were familiar friends, because, through the kindness of Mrs. Malcolm and her uncle, I had been hearing so much about the artist. I seemed to see in my mind's eye the house on Trenton Street about which I had heard, with the bees swarming out from under the roof on their journey to gather honey, and the whole family party starting forth from the front door on a quest for possible patrons who might want their portraits painted. More than that, I could visualize William Prior standing before his easel and painting the two portraits (pages 20 and 21) which I had just found. Both of these portraits are painted in the technique of the Fall River-Sturbridge School of Painting.

As I said before, Prior made a practice of grinding his own paints. As a result they never faded, but remained brilliant. Even those portraits which were left in the dust and cobwebs of an old damp garret for years needed only to be cleaned and varnished to emerge unfaded and as colorful as the day on which they were painted. It must be said that he was not alone in this, for it was the general habit of the itinerant artists, just as it was the habit of the old masters on the other side of the water, and we know how wonderful the colors are on their masterpieces.

The young man in question had grey-blue eyes and light brown curly hair. He was probably still in his teens, for his cheeks are pink, and there is a smile in the corner of his eye that is very challenging. His black coat shows up well against a grey background, and his brown waistcoat enlivened by thin yellow stripes and the greyish-brown cravat tied with quite an artistic abandon give one an inkling that he might develop into a dandy later on. The background is a soft grey. The portrait is signed, 'William M. Prior, New Bedford, Mass.'

The portrait of the old lady with her glasses on was painted in 1844. The subject, of course, has not the subtle attraction of the other. Just the same, she is a nice old lady, smart and up-and-coming, as they say in the country. She is a Mrs. Chase of South Dennis, Massachusetts. The grey background of the picture has a red curtain across it, to cheer it up, and against it her nut-brown wig, or 'brown front' as it was called, stands out in full relief, just as do the black rims of her spectacles against her plump, florid cheeks. Her black velvet dress and muslin kerchief and cap give her a fine air of eminent respectability, and make her perfectly typical of her day and age. The 'brown front' was a recognized part of every elderly lady's costume in those days. No one thought of having grey hair or thin hair. If they reached a certain time of life when the hair was not satisfactory to look at, they donned the brown front, and it was taken as a matter of course.

Now, in contrast to these portraits of the Fall River-Sturbridge style of painting, I was fortunate enough to acquire a portrait (page 22) of 'H. B. Webb, Esq., Shipbuilder,' signed by 'Prior, Bath, Maine.' This is a fine example of his earlier style of painting and is exceedingly well done. It was painted by William Matthew Prior in 1831. The two styles, however, bear absolutely no resemblance to each other. H. B. Webb, Esq., Shipbuilder, has dark brown hair, and very expressive brown eyes. He wears a black coat with a velvet collar and a white silk choker. The grey background merges into a dull red at the foot of the canvas.

In regard to this Fall River-Sturbridge School of Painting everyone is very vague as to its origin, but it would seem very certain that William M. Prior was the instigator of it. He did more painting in both these towns at that time than anyone else did as far as it can be ascertained, and his change of style was so sudden that it would seem to be beyond question that he was the leader of it, for others followed him, and it became a distinct branch of the painting of the day.

I made a pilgrimage to Sturbridge to see if I could get any information about this old Fall River-Sturbridge style of painting. I went to the public library thinking that would be the most likely place to begin my search. To my great disappointment, I could find no trace of anything there. The librarians, two of them, were very young women of foreign extraction. They knew nothing about the old days of Sturbridge or its traditions. Then I went to some of the older people in the place, and they told me there was no one now living who could give me any information on the subject. All those who might have helped me had passed on, and the place was greatly changed. No one there or anywhere else seems to be able to answer the question. One comes across portraits now and then that belong to that school. I secured four of them from Sturbridge. These are not by Prior. They are of the Fall River-Sturbridge School of Painting, but in its more glorified form. They far outdo Prior in technique and importance, but the artist is unknown. To find out his name has been one of the main reasons for my trips to Sturbridge which ended in so much disappointment. But that does not mean that the name will never be discovered. It may turn up at any time, in some unexpected way.

These portraits demonstrate the style of painting to a marked degree. (Pages 23 and 24.) The coloring and the attention paid to detail are worthy of some of the old Dutch pictures. The embroidered muslin and the materials are so true to life that one feels like touching them to see if they are real. It will be noticed that there is practically no shading in the faces. They are painted in flat colors, and yet they stand out well.

One interesting feature is the manner of painting husband and wife in such a way that they could be framed together, side by side. The backgrounds dovetail into each other and form a continuous garden scene or wood scene or whatever the artist had in mind against which to place his subjects. In the case of this first couple it was a stone pillar and balustrade against a landscape with blue skies and green trees. A dull pink curtain partially shields this. The woman has a fair complexion and brown hair with high lights in it, which show up against a very delicate tortoise-shell comb such as our grandmothers used to wear. She is young and pretty, and though somewhat stiff and woodeny, she has quite a little air to her and is of the very feminine type which was so much admired in her day. She wears a black satin dress with bunches of embossed velvet flowers scattered over it. Her gold filigree earrings are painted with a great devotion to detail, as well as her gold rings, gold chain, ivory brooch with gold setting, and the vest, collar, and sleeves of muslin, exquisitely embroidered. Her blue eyes match the blue of the sky in the background. Many of the younger visitors to the picture gallery have stood before this picture in admiration exclaiming that it might have been painted by one of the modern French artists. And yet there it is, at least one hundred years old, primitive in its conception, yet with a charm of coloring and a truthfulness of execution that surprises one.

Her husband is rather a pompous young man. He has the same fair skin, but his hair is light and his eyes are almost china blue. The same background of stone pillar, sky, and woods are back of him. The same dull pink curtain merging into red behind the arms partially shields them. Evidently if his wife loved pretty clothes, he ran neck to neck with her. He looks as though he had come right out of a fashionable tailor establishment of that period. His coat has evidently just been pressed, and has not the sign of a crease in it. It is of black broadcloth with a wide satin collar. His tucked white shirt is immaculate, as is his broad satin cravat or stock. He holds a book in his hand. The way in which the hands are painted is quite unique. I have never come across any like them. All four of the portraits have these same hands, though posed differently, and it is evident that the same artist painted them.

In studying and analyzing the degrees of excellence amongst these itinerant artists, who all started without instruction of any kind, one can more or less gauge the point they have reached on the road of portrait painting by many things they have left out rather than what they have put in. For instance, those who never got beyond doing more or less crude work were very shy about painting the tips of fingers of the hands of their sitters. They hid them under the leaves of a book, or their fingers were turned in and only the backs of the hands showed. As for thumbs — those were in most cases strictly avoided. The hands of these portraits in question, while rigid and rather lifeless, were done with the utmost care as to detail. The nails were all painted just so, suggestive of a Japanese painting, which differs very much from most portraits of the time that border on the primitive. The artist, whoever he was, had a certain gift for drawing, and it was not only the hands that were dealt with in that way, but almost every eyelash can be counted, and all the filigree work in the pieces of jewelry and the texture of the clothes and the details in the lace were painted with the same accuracy and care. These characteristics in regard to hands can be found among the old pre-Raphaelite artists of Italy. In fact, it is curious to note that the primitive artists of all time seem to meet with the same difficulties and to use the same methods regardless of the country or period to which they belong.

The second couple from Sturbridge is painted (pages 25 and 26), like the others, in the Fall River-Sturbridge School of Painting. It has the same well-groomed characteristics of the first couple. Every detail in their costumes had been attended to. The woman has almost black hair, clear brown eyes with black eyebrows well defined. Her cheeks are delicately pink. She wears a black velvet dress with puffed sleeves. Around her neck is a beautiful ruffle attached to a guimpe of point d'esprit lace. On her lustrous black hair she wears a cap of embroidered muslin exquisitely painted. Pink ruffles surround the crown, and gauze ribbons striped with pink fall down from the cap on each side of her face and on down to her dress. She sits with her elbow leaning on a dull pink chair. A filigree ring is on her forefinger. She is very pretty to look at, and her eyes are very speaking as they look out from the canvas. The background is reddish-brown.

Her husband sits against the same reddish-brown background, but in this case it is lightened around the head, which gives it almost the look of a halo, but there is nothing ethereal about him. On the contrary, he wears a very smart black velvet coat, with a rolling collar, and a white satin stock in which there is a gold stickpin with a pink stone in the centre. The stock is wrapped around his throat with the two points of the collar showing in front. He has dark brown hair and blue eyes, and is sitting at a table which is painted red, on which there is an open book with part of the title visible, 'The Pleasures of ——, Part 1st.' He is using a quill pen on a broad sheet of paper on which there is some writing, but it is so small and illegible that I doubt if anybody could make it out.

One cannot help feeling in seeing the portraits of these two young couples that probably those days were no different from these days where the young married set dominates the social element of the towns. It is very evident in looking at both these couples that they were quite ready to enjoy themselves, and that gives one a certain sense of relief from the impression that is so prevalent that everyone had long faces, and laughter was a sin, and a pretty dress nothing but vanity.

The same may be said of John and Mary Williams of Pepperell, Massachusetts, although they put up a stiffer appearance for the general public to see. (Page 27.) The fact that they have a background of trees and open air behind them indicates a great similarity of thought on the part of both artists. This painting, however, is very decidedly a primitive. The artist evidently had a similar conception of hands and the method of painting them, only these are less shapely and less lifelike; but the nails are carefully done, and the fingers are as pointed. The background is made up of a country scene. There is a house in it, with lights in the windows and smoke coming out of the chimney, which gives a comfortable suggestion to the picture of home and fireside. John wears a black velvet coat, black satin waistcoat speckled with red dots, and high black choker. He has black hair and hazel eyes, and sits very straight, and hasn't the sign of a smile on his face. Sometimes those are the kind that are the gayest dancers in the Barn Dance!

Mary, his wife, sits against that same background. She has on a black velvet dress with a muslin collar. She holds a dull red book in her hand. Her carroty-red corkscrew curls bunched on either side of her face are a marvel to look upon. Her skin is fair and her eyes are brown, and her waist is very small. She, like John, looks as though butter would not melt in her mouth, but the whole picture has a unique charm, because it is the best type of a primitive, and depicts the characteristics of the couple so vividly that you come back to look at it more than once.

There is one thing that the itinerant artists excelled in, and that is the painting of lace and embroideries. Any housewife who had a bit of fine lace on her cap or on her kerchief took good care to have it in the picture, for anything of that nature was handed down from generation to generation, until finally it became an heirloom. The painting of jewelry was also an art they excelled in, and Grandmother's cameo breastpin could be pointed to with pride by her grandchild who inherited it, when showing the portrait to someone years after the old lady had passed away. It has been said by some that those who were so successful in painting lace and jewelry were those who had begun by working on tavern signs and coaches on which delicate and intricate coats-of-arms were frequently painted. This also could be said of many of the materials the sitters wore which showed the texture of satin and velvet — the crispness of muslin stocks, the cloth coats of the men, etc. — to a marked degree.

The portraits of John and Mary Williams of Pepperell, Massachusetts, were framed together like one panel, with a strip of gold frame separating them. That was the way these portraits of couples with out-of-door backgrounds were supposed to be framed, only the farmhouses were not big enough to devote that amount of space to them, and in that case they were framed separately and hung near each other.

Before closing this chapter I will include the accompanying portrait of a woman painted by G. Alden. (Page 28.) This artist was an enthusiastic follower of William M. Prior. As to whether he is any relation to Noah Alden, the artist, is something I have not been able to find out. He was evidently one of those who adopted the Fall River-Sturbridge School of Painting.

But to return once more to William M. Prior. As old age came on, times were changing, the daguerreotype began to be very popular. Whether it was that or because he was getting older that business was less good, one cannot say, but he found it very fatiguing to make these distant trips. He had made one to Baltimore which taxed his strength a good deal, and he painted a great many pictures there, which was exceedingly gratifying to him, but when he returned he took things more slowly, and he began to paint portraits on glass, as we said before, and also on the glass doors over the old-fashioned clocks made to hide the pendulums. He lived to be sixty-six years old, and died in Boston in January, 1873, and was listed in the Boston Directory of 1841 as a portrait painter of East Boston. It also mentioned that he owned a house there which was still in his possession when he died.

It may be interesting to some to learn that he was descended from Benjamin Prior, who came from England to Duxbury in 1638. This gentleman was Prior's great-great-great-grandfather, whose brother Matthew became Poet Laureate of England during the reign of Queen Elizabeth, and was buried in Westminster Abbey. Though Prior himself died in East Boston, he was buried in Woodlawn Cemetery in Everett, Massachusetts.

CHAPTER III

THERE is no doubt that the painting of children is one of the most difficult things an artist can undertake to do. Even the greatest of them have slipped down miserably in attempting it. Their painting of adults can be everything that one could desire, yet, when they come to painting children, they seem to be at a loss. That being the case, the derision hurled at some of the portraits of children painted by the old itinerant portrait painters, who never had any instructions of any kind to help them along, seems uncalled for. While there are many that have a rather grotesque look, there are again a great many that are exceedingly well done and show imagination and charm, but at best it is no easy matter.

Different artists had different methods. Having found that it was practically impossible to keep children quiet, some took to drawing the bodies before undertaking to paint any other part of the portrait, and then managed to paint the head in from life as quickly as they could. Others sketched out the figure of the child, and after blocking in some of the colors dismissed the little restless creature and finished the painting in quiet and peace of mind. When that was done, the child was called back and cajoled as much as possible into keeping still enough for the head to be painted in.

Still another method was to start out on a journey for procuring patrons with a full line of figures of children already painted on canvases which had been finished in their own homes. They offered a varied assortment. Little boys usually held a whip, a rabbit, or a toy of some kind. The little girls held a nosegay or a basket of flowers. Some even went so far as to have a kitten in the child's arms. There were many of these designs from which the patron could choose, and they could be changed at will if need be. If Johnny had a pet dog, the dog could easily be painted over the original painting, and it need not show, or if little Elmira had a pet canary bird, that too could be treated in the same manner.

The children of that period were singularly bound in by systems of decorum, if one can judge by the postures they were put in. Among other requirements, both little boys and little girls were taught to turn their toes out to an extreme angle, not only when learning to dance, or walking across the room, but all the time, which is, after all, quite unnatural and exceedingly bad for the posture of the body, according to modern science. Children had to sit bolt upright in their chairs, and never lean back. The chairs had wooden backs, so it would not have helped them much if they had. They were never allowed to lounge. Therefore, it is not strange that some of the portraits one finds look more or less either like the old-fashioned Dutch dolls which were made of wood and jointed, or like anemic specimens of childhood apparently too feeble to live long. This was largely due to the conservative theories of the time. Many thought a sickly hue to the faces was interesting, and did not mind if the bodies looked dislocated.

I once went into a house where I saw the picture of a little girl hanging on the wall that literally made me shudder. The hands and feet were as small as those of a doll, and the head was twice as big as in life. The color of its little face was a sickly yellowish-grey. I was told that it was painted after the child had died, and the artist had received the descriptions of her from various members of the family. The result was appalling. But from what I gathered, the mother had valued it very highly. I understood, however, that she was a strangely unwholesome and morbid sort of woman, as was sometimes to be found in old farmhouses of New England. It appears that her favorite song was:

> 'Only a little baby girl
> Dead by the riverside.'

This, of course, was an extreme case.

Fortunately, one comes across portraits of children that look healthy and robust and have something of the atmosphere of childhood about them. It is well to recall that in visiting the famous galleries of Europe, one finds many portraits of children with that same anemic coloring and lack of correct drawing, and these are by some of the greatest artists of the old school. Portraits of children by the pre-Raphaelite masters abound in such specimens, and yet the public gazes on them apparently with breathless admiration. But there is often a reason for this, because, in spite of the lack of drawing and the death-like coloring, the artist has in some way made life emanate from the picture. There is a certain something about it, perhaps one might call it 'atmosphere,' that makes one only conscious of the vitality of the imagination that conceived it. Apparently the inaccuracies of the drawing and the coloring do not seem always to matter.

One day in my wanderings, I came across a picture (page 61) of three children by Benjamin F. Nutting, a little girl and her two younger brothers. This was a good example of the artist's having painted the bodies first and put the heads on afterwards, the result being that none of the heads really fit to the bodies, and in order to give a gracious expression to them, they were all somewhat tilted to one side, producing a look of affectation that could not be surpassed.

One gentleman from San Francisco wrote to me in regard to this matter of painting the bodies first and filling in with the heads afterwards. 'I own two oil paintings of ancestors which were in my attic at Littleton for many years, before I resurrected them and took them to New York with me,' he writes. 'I was always told they were done by an itinerant portrait painter who came to the town with a load of canvases. The theory was that everything was painted before he struck town except for an oval left where the particular face was to go. The portraits I have are of a man and a woman. In the case of the man particularly it is easy to imagine this oval space where the head was added, for it looks a little "skewgee"!'

Benjamin Nutting painted a great many portraits in Boston and in many towns and villages in the state. I received the following letter about him from a lady living in Westford, Massachusetts. She wrote as follows:

'Many weeks ago I read your notice in the "Westford Wardsman," but illness in the family prevented me from answering it until this time. Perhaps the little information I am able to give you will be of no value, but several who have seen my portraits said I should write to you. Two of them are by B. F. Nutting, Pt. 1858. My grandmother was in Newbury, Vermont, at the time my grandfather was principal of the Academy there. Their first four children were born in Newbury, my father, in 1853.

'Father cannot recall anything in connection with the portraits, but grandmother always had the four, her two boys and her two girls, hanging in her room, and the two boys now belong to me. The work is well done and quite true to life, as daguerreotypes in the family show. I have had some excellent photographs made of the four portraits and will be happy for you to see them or the originals if they can help you in any way.

'I am much interested in these early portrait painters, and hope you are planning for a book.

'Sincerely,
'(Signed) Mrs. ——'

I went over to Westford to see the lady and the portraits. I was well repaid in doing this. They were much more natural than the portrait I mentioned above, but the style of painting was very similar. Nutting's painting was very good according to the standards of those days, and these portraits at Westford were evidently done with a great deal of care. There are one or two points of similarity in all his paintings of children. The mouths are always like Cupid's bows and the nostrils make the little noses look rather pinched. The shoulders are always very square, and the flesh tints are noticeably anemic.

After seeing them I became interested to know what Nutting was like as a man. I received word from two ladies living in Harvard that if I wanted to know anything about Benjamin F. Nutting, they could tell me something about him, and they asked me to go to see them. I found them living in a fascinating little house, one of the earliest in Harvard, and full of heirlooms. We sat down in the old-fashioned parlor and began to talk of Benjamin Nutting. One of these ladies told me that very many years ago she had taken water-color lessons of him, when she was a young girl. He had then become too old to be an itinerant artist. He had a small room which he called his studio on West Street in Boston, where he gave lessons in water-color. She said he was very old and a little bit of a man at that time, extremely thin and wizened-looking, with long bony hands and flowing white chin beard. His hair also was snowy white and hung down upon his shoulders, which gave him the appearance of a Luna moth. She said he had quite a number of pupils, and was a very good teacher.

After a pause she went on with her description. 'Benjamin Nutting was not of the vigorous type,' she said. 'Like his portraits, which were painted in delicate colors, he was non-dynamic. He moved about his studio like a shadow and his voice was thin and quavery. He paid great attention to the manner of handling the paint brush, and insisted upon a long, sweeping movement that insured smooth, brilliant colors. The pity of it was, that after working hard all of his life, and having painted many portraits acceptable to the sitters, he died in extreme poverty at a great age, having returned to Watertown, from whence he had come, and was cared for by a kind landlady named Mrs. Philbrook.'

The ladies I had gone to see were very kind, and became very much interested in my researches. They wrote to an aged uncle of theirs asking him if he had any recollections of Benjamin F. Nutting. An answer came shortly from Minneapolis, Minnesota. 'I can't tell you much of Mr. Nutting,' he wrote. 'His studio was over the architect's office I was in, and I took lessons in water-colors of him, and it was there I met A—— in '73. We had some water-colors of his, and have now. A—— knew him very well, but I only casually. He was a quiet man with a full beard. Some of those old portraits of his were very well painted, but not signed. I have two. They are of A——'s grandparents. Miss Sears may find out something about Mr. Nutting from the Federation of Arts at Washington, D.C.'

I found this out. Benjamin F. Nutting was a contemporary of Currier of old-prints fame, who was born in 1813. The former never married. At one time he had business dealings with Williams and Everett, art dealers, in Boston. He left a number of his paintings in his cottage on the easterly side of Fayette Street, in Watertown, Massachusetts. It would be interesting to know their fate.

When I returned from Westford, I took the first opportunity to go to see the picture of the three children I had seen before, and found it such a perfectly fine example of what could happen when heads were painted a little bit askew, and it demonstrated my point so well, that I decided to add it to the collection at Harvard, Massachusetts, for educational purposes.

Having learned that Nutting was a water-colorist as well as a painter in oils, I could now see that it accounted for the flat look of his pictures, for he put his oil paints on just as he would have done had he been painting in water-colors, with broad splashes of color. The little girl in the picture is dressed in delicate blue, the oldest boy in a brownish suit with a black belt and holding a toy whip in one hand. He has a ruffle of lace around his neck. The girl has dark hair and the two boys are fair. The smaller boy wears a yellowish silk dress edged with lace. It was a curious thing in those days and the days preceding them and for quite a period afterwards that little boys were dressed in the same manner as little girls, so you could hardly tell the difference between the two. There were apt to be curls framing each side of the face, one curl sometimes tied by a ribbon. The dresses were cut low in the neck with little frills around them. There seemed to be a desire on the part of the mothers not to let the boyish proclivities show themselves until they could no longer be hidden. These small boys in this particular picture were an exception, for they had their hair cut short and parted on the side, and were it not for the yellowish silk dress edged with lace on the small boy, one would have thought what fine little men they were.

There is a tradition that wise old Solomon of Biblical days boasted that he could distinguish small boys from small girls. Some of his subjects, however, questioned this, for they were dressed alike. He commanded that a group of both sexes be brought before him and given a basin of water. When this was done, they were told to wash their hands. Immediately the small boys began to roll up their sleeves, and King Solomon pointed to them with pride and uttered the one word 'boys.' This goes to show that even in those days this particular habit of dressing small boys and girls alike was in vogue.

I own some old-fashioned daguerreotypes of children posed

and dressed in a fashion similar to these children painted by
Nutting. It seems the French at that time thought the
fashion a charming one. They called it 'suave' and 'gentil'
and 'mignon'!

Nutting is listed in the *Dictionary of American Painters,
Sculptors, and Engravers*, by Mantle Fielding, as a 'portrait
painter who worked in Boston from 1826 to 1884. He also
drew on stone for the lithographers.'

One day shortly after this, I went to an old house in
Littleton, Massachusetts, and looked at a picture I had seen
on the walls there for many years. I had always been mysti-
fied by it because, though I could see that it was of a little
girl, there was such a peculiar film over it that she had almost
disappeared from sight. At that time the artist of the picture
was unknown, and in fact no one seemed to know very much
about the picture except that it was of a little girl named
Lottie Reed. I began to ask questions about it, and finally
was able to acquire it of the owner of the house. I was anxious
to see what the portrait would look like if this thick milky
film were removed from it. (Page 62.)

Lottie Reed was born and brought up in the old picturesque
town of Sterling, Massachusetts. When she grew up, she
married a man named Lucien Priest of Littleton and thereafter
was always known as Lottie Priest. She was a daughter of
Mr. Levi Reed of Sterling, and let me say here that he must
have been a quaint old gentleman. One of the still living
relatives told me the following anecdote about him:

At one time he had his house painted when he was a very
old man and the windows got stuck so that the one at which
he was accustomed to sit could not be opened. The glass got a
little bit dimmed and he would put both his hands up to his
eyes as though he were using opera glasses and would peer out
to see what he could see along the village street. When he
saw someone coming he would call out to his wife in a shrill
voice: 'Sally! Sally! Who is this passing by?' This happened

so often that finally his wife and whoever happened to be with her paid no attention to him. When this was the case, and they did not come to his aid, he would then fall back in his chair, shrug his shoulders impatiently, and exclaim, or rather shout, 'Don't know, don't care, don't give a damn!' so all the village could hear him.

He had his own ideas about food. He was asked one day if he would partake of watermelon. 'No! I'll be damned if I do,' he cried. 'You don't catch me eating those new-fangled things! They never had 'em in my day!' He was ninety-two years old at this time.

It did not take long before the portrait of Lottie Priest was returned with its opaque covering removed, and I was delighted and amazed to find revealed the interesting picture of a child well painted and well drawn. The paint was, as the restorer said, 'as fresh as it was on the day it was put on.' The waxy film covering it had thoroughly protected it for well over a century.

There was a very strange thing about the picture — the child had only one arm. The sleeve was there, all ready to contain that member, but the arm was lacking. I asked as many people about it as I thought would have any knowledge of it in Sterling and Littleton, Massachusetts, but they could give no reason for it.

I found the house where Lottie Priest had lived during her childhood. It was a very old and picturesque house and looked out upon the Sterling Common, shaded by giant elm trees. There were two or three descendants still living there, but they had no information to give me about the portrait except that it was always a question as to who had painted it.

It was a curious coincidence that in one of my wanderings around Fitchburg, Massachusetts, a lady there told me a very amusing anecdote about a neighbor of her mother's who had had a group portrait of three of her children painted by a very erratic man from Sterling. His name was Jones Fawson Morris. The three children were very close together as regards age, and she was anxious to get a perfect likeness of them. Now, the trouble with this erratic portrait painter was that he had a way of over-consoling himself when he was about to paint a portrait. She knew this, but she thought that perhaps she might escape any perilous experience. The day came and he appeared on the scene, arranged his easel, got out his paints, posed the children, and the first sitting began. All went well except that Mrs. L—— had a very nervous feeling that he was not quite himself.

The following sittings went on the same, each time clearly showing him to be somewhat under the effects of his consolation, until on one occasion he said that he would not put the eyes in until the next sitting, which happened to be the following day. The lady felt quite uneasy about it and awaited his arrival with some misgivings. When he walked up the pathway to the door, it was more than evident that he was very much affected; in fact, he was in a state of intoxication. To make matters worse he demanded more drink. Mrs. L—— was so afraid of angering him that she nervously gave him a large gobletful, which he drank with avidity, and then, to her dismay, he went into the sitting-room and sank down upon the floor in a heap! She did not feel that he was in any condition to paint in the eyes of her children, but he insisted upon doing so, and would not listen to her, but told her to bring the canvas close to him and prop it up against the sofa. The children stood up in a row before him, speechless with astonishment, while their poor mother covered her face with her hand, terrified by the possibility of their likenesses passing down to posterity squint-eyed, wall-eyed, blear-eyed, or possibly even cross-eyed. In fact, her imagination knew no bounds as to what might happen under these circumstances.

In the meantime the artist struggled to his knees, and held on to the sofa to keep himself steady. Then he began to

PORTRAIT OF THREE CHILDREN OF NEWBURY, VERMONT
Painted by Benjamin F. Nutting in 1840.
(Description, page 53)

[61]

PORTRAIT OF LOTTIE REED OF STERLING, MASSACHUSETTS
Painted by Jones Fawson Morris about 1840.
(Description, pages 58, 59)

PORTRAIT OF A BOY WITH RED SHOES
Artist's signature 'J.H.M.' Painted in June, 1832.
(Description, pages 78, 79)

PORTRAIT OF MARY ELIZA JENKINS
Painted by Isaac A. Wetherbee in 1843.
(Description, page 79)

PORTRAIT OF WILLIAM HENRY GORHAM OF SPRINGFIELD,
MASSACHUSETTS
Painted by William S. Elwell in 1842.
(Description, page 80)

PORTRAIT OF A LITTLE GIRL IN A RED DRESS
Painted by Joseph Goodhue Chandler in 1840.
(Description, page 81)

[66]

PORTRAIT OF CLINTON HAGER OF WESTMINSTER, MASSACHUSETTS

Painted in 1843, probably by Deacon Robert Peckham. (Presented to this Collection by the Board of Trustees of the Furbush Memorial Library of Westminster.)

(Description, page 83)

[67]

PORTRAIT OF CHARLES L. EATON AND HIS SISTER OF BOSTON,
MASSACHUSETTS

Painted by J. Harvey Young in 1848. (*This was painted in Young's itinerant days.*)
(Description, page 85)

PORTRAIT OF SARAH AMANDA BENNETT
Painted by Jeremiah L. Harding in 1839.
(Description, page 86)

PORTRAIT OF ELIZA BENNETT
Painted by Jeremiah L. Harding in 1839.
(Description, page 86)

PORTRAIT OF A CHILD FROM HANCOCK, NEW HAMPSHIRE
Painted by H. Bundy in 1850.
(Description, page 87)

PORTRAIT OF HENRY MUNRO AND HIS TWIN BROTHER
Painted by Ferdinand T. L. Boyle.
(Description, page 87)

PORTRAIT OF A LITTLE GIRL WITH A CURL ON HER FOREHEAD
Artist unknown.
(Description, page 88)

PORTRAIT OF A LITTLE GIRL IN A BLUE DRESS FROM
MASSACHUSETTS
Artist unknown. Painted about 1840.
(Description, pages 88, 89)

PORTRAIT OF THREE CHILDREN FROM MASSACHUSETTS
Artist unknown.
(Description, page 89)

PORTRAIT OF ALOYISHUS BROWN OF GRAFTON, MASSACHUSETTS
Artist unknown.
(Description, pages 89, 90)

squeeze paint onto his palette, and wielding a paint brush in the air he began the difficult process of painting in the eyes. Mrs. L—— sat most of the time shielding her face with her hand. She was greatly distressed. Whenever she gained courage enough to peer out between her fingers it seemed to her that the artist's paint brush was acting in an irresponsible and terrifyingly erratic manner, touching the canvas in a hit-or-miss way apparently without rhyme or reason. Every now and then he sank from his knees to a sitting posture, and regained his balance with great difficulty.

Finally, after what seemed a long time, he declared the picture finished, and Mrs. L—— hardly dared to look at it. When she brought her mind to doing so, to her amazement she found the eyes of her children were exceedingly well done, full of expression and clear. She did not know what to say to him. The relief was tremendous. She had had visions of being obliged to destroy the picture when the artist had left, but now she found herself in possession of a very good and apparently normal portrait of her children, of which she could be proud.

Some of this I learned from her grandson who inherited the portrait. He prized it very much, not only for itself, for there was something very quaint and spontaneous about it, but also for the unique tale attached to it. The lady who told me a part of this said that she knew the painting was still in existence and that she could find out for me the name of the grandson who had inherited it. She said he lived in Boston. I entered into communication with him and he said that the story was quite true, and that if I cared to see the picture he would be very glad to show it to me, so I went to see it. It was quite an attractive portrait of three children, but what I noticed especially was the fresh brilliancy of the coloring. I asked this gentleman if the picture had been restored in any way, and he said no. The more I examined it, the more I became absolutely sure that the artist who painted it was the same who had painted the portrait of Lottie Reed of Sterling, now in my possession. There was no mistaking it.

Then I asked him more about this man, Jones Fawson Morris. He said that he was baptized in Leominster, but lived in Sterling and had done a good deal of painting in and about that locality around 1835–1840. Then I became convinced that he had undoubtedly been consoling himself when he had painted the portrait of Lottie Reed and had left it unfinished, just as he had left the portrait of Mrs. L——'s children, promising to come back the next day; only in the case of Lottie Reed he had not come back, and therefore she had to face future generations with only one arm. She died in 1908 at seventy-four years of age.

I made a special visit to Sterling when I was told that there was a portrait by Jones Fawson Morris in the Sterling Library. I found it hanging on the wall upstairs surrounded by many portraits of long-deceased town fathers. This particular one was a portrait of a man named Moses Thomas. I then saw that when it had been painted Morris must have been absolutely sober, for it was a perfectly uninteresting and muddy specimen, and the technique of the others I had seen was completely lacking. Therefore, I came to the conclusion that what I had heard in the old town was true, that Morris was one of the artists who could do his best only when under the influence of liquor.

To pass on to another picture (page 63) in the collection, there is a portrait of a boy that has puzzled many who have looked at it, for the artist's signature is not written in full, but he signs himself 'J.H.M., June, 1832.' The boy is in a blue dress with red shoes and lies half-recumbent on the grass, his back leaning against the brown trunk of a forest tree, one hand resting upon a bright red bag of the same color as his shoes. The background on one side is a landscape of mountainous country which one sees through the green leaves of the tree. The boy has light brown curly hair and blue eyes.

[78]

One suspects that the artist had seen an illustration of a portrait by Sir Joshua Reynolds and that this style of painting had become fixed in his mind and he unconsciously followed it. In any case he was evidently deeply affected by the English School of Painting. Those who have seen it admire it very much, and the signature 'J.H.M.' usually starts a controversy, some people thinking it may be one artist and some believing it may be another. If anyone reading this should have more definite knowledge of this subject, I should be very glad to hear of it. There is enough about the picture, however, to make one feel sure that its author came under the category of self-made artists who were wandering about the countryside in search of patrons.

One day I received word from a lady living in Melrose who told me that she had a number of family portraits, and if I would like to see them, she would be glad to show them to me. I had come into possession of an unusually attractive portrait (page 64) of a little girl named Mary Eliza Jenkins, painted by Isaac A. Wetherbee in 1843. Shortly after acquiring it I received the aforesaid letter. This portrait of Mary Eliza had been in the lady's possession as that of one of her ancestors. She certainly had a most interesting collection of many generations back, which I enjoyed seeing, but the picture of Mary Eliza had a quaint charm to it that was especially appealing. She is a little fair-haired girl, with half-moon curls on her forehead, and brown eyes, dressed in white watered satin with white pantalettes. In her extended hand she holds a gay bunch of flowers. Under her little black slippers is an old-fashioned Brussels carpet with geometrical designs on it. Behind her is a red curtain. She came of an old New England family, and to show how deeply engraved are the characteristics of the housekeepers of the olden days, I was told that her great-grandmother in having a thorough spring cleaning of her house removed the glass protecting two beautiful portraits in pastel of her grandparents, and proceeded to dust them off briskly. In so doing she brushed away much of the detail, and when the family saw it, they threw up their hands in dismay. It was truly a great pity, for the portraits were by Doyle and were of great personal value to them.

It is quite evident that Isaac A. Wetherbee was in great demand during the years of his portrait painting, for specimens of his work have found their way to far-distant states. There is a certain elegance to the portraits he painted, and he was never unflattering to the sitter, which accounts for a good deal in the long run. Most of his paintings were done in the eighteen-forties. In 1842 he exhibited them in the Athenaeum Gallery in Boston.

One of the very prominent itinerant artists associated with Springfield, Massachusetts, was William S. Elwell. He began his career in Hartford, Connecticut, and is listed as being there in a house in the rear of Temple Street in 1839. From there he went to Springfield, where he was living in a cottage on Maple Street in 1845. His paintings are something entirely different from those known as primitives. It seems that he never went through the primitive period, but by instinct started out following along conventional lines. He had great natural talent, and it is said that when he had collected sufficient funds he went and studied under Chester Harding.

I have come across only one picture of Elwell's, and was fortunate enough to be able to add it to the collection at Harvard, Massachusetts. It is a portrait (page 65) of William Henry Gorham, hardly more than three years old. It is a very lovely picture of a little boy sitting on the ground. In one hand he holds a toy whip which rests on a red footstool. In the other he clutches a red rose with green leaves. His dress is also red and soft in coloring. A vase of flowers melts into the background at the right. He has light hair and brown eyes, and the whole picture has a mellow, harmonious atmosphere that is restful and attractive.

Elwell was born in Brimfield, Massachusetts, in 1810 and

died in Springfield in 1881. A rough granite boulder marks his grave, which is near that of Chester Harding. In 1848 he painted the portrait of Dolly Madison, which was said to be very lovely.

Still another type of portraits of children was that of a child in a red dress curled up in a big armchair, painted by Joseph Goodhue Chandler in 1840. (Page 66.) This artist was born in South Hadley, Massachusetts, in 1813. He was one of those who accumulated sufficient funds to make a study of his profession, and he worked for a short time under William Collins of Albany. After wandering about, painting portraits wherever he could, he took a room in Boston which he called a studio. He was very fortunate in developing his talent along the right lines, and finally became prominent, so much so that he painted a portrait of Daniel Webster of which he made thirty copies and sold them all.

The name of the child he painted in the red dress is not known. The portrait is exceedingly well painted. The background of the picture is of greyish-brown. The little girl's dress has ruffles on it. Her white pantalettes peep out from under it. Her little fat hand holds a blue flower with green leaves. She wears her hair in long brown curls, and her eyes are dark blue. A coral necklace is wound around her neck and she is sitting in a green stuffed chair. The hands are well done and shapely.

The artist, Joseph Goodhue Chandler, married Lucretia Waite in 1840. He died in Hubbardston, Massachusetts, and is buried in Greenwood Cemetery.

One day I went over to the old town of Westminster, Massachusetts, because I was following the trail of one of the itinerant artists who was well known throughout the state. His name was Robert Peckham, and he was always known as old Deacon Peckham of Westminster. After the death of his wife he lived there all the rest of his life with his maiden sister in a dear old-fashioned house on the highway. I tried to get a photograph of it several times with my camera, but it was so surrounded with maple trees that I could not catch a glimpse of it that would in any way show what it was like. It was typical of one of the old New England houses of the better type with a white picket fence around it and a lilac bush or two in the front yard.

I asked in the public library if anybody in the town could give me any information about Peckham. One of the librarians spoke up and said that her mother remembered him as a very old man with long grey hair reaching to his shoulders, and as he passed down the road to his home he looked just like the old man in Oliver Wendell Holmes's poem 'The Last Leaf.' They asked me to go upstairs to see the collection of Deacon Peckham's portraits, which he had painted of some of the old residents in Westminster. There were ten of them in all. I was exceedingly interested in seeing them. They were, to be sure, somewhat stiff and woodeny, but like most of the work of the itinerant painters they convinced one that the likeness of each was good. They had character and a certain amount of distinction. The artist had a strong, sure touch with his paint brush. The colors were all clear and distinct. Some of the sitters were less stiff than others, and none of them had been what one might call 'worked over.' The bits of lace in the different portraits were beautifully painted.

The librarian was very much interested in showing me these, and I kept asking her whether there were not others for me to see. We started on a voyage of discovery. Opening a secluded closet we looked in, and saw a portrait with its face turned to the wall at the farther end. I asked her what it was, and she said she had only a vague idea because she had not looked at it for a very long time. She thought it was a portrait of a young boy whose father had sent it to the library when he felt his life was soon coming to an end. He died so suddenly that the information regarding it was very meagre, but they had found out that the boy was this gentleman's son, and that he had died about two years before his father, who was born in Westminster but had gone away to one of the big cities; they had lost track of him until this portrait had suddenly arrived, and that happened a great many years ago. They were of the opinion that it was painted by old Deacon Peckham. Unfortunately it was unsigned, like most of the portraits of that time.

After I had been told all this, we drew it out of the closet. The dust of ages had accumulated upon it. The librarian got a cloth and gently removed as much of it as she could. Then we saw a most delightful portrait (page 67) of a young boy, beautifully painted and in perfect drawing. It had great imagination and charm to it. The boy is dressed in black with a broad white muslin ruff around his neck. He holds a little book in his hand. His face has rather unusual characteristics to it, and his light brown hair is shot with gold and is full of life. The portrait is very suggestive of Spanish paintings and in a crude way has a resemblance to some of Velasquez's portraits, especially of the Infanta of Spain. The treatment of the brow and the shape of the head and the whole contour of the face and body bring to mind the Spanish influence in art. Probably the old deacon (if it was painted by him) had seen some illustration of a Spanish work of art that had impressed him and the influence of it worked its way into the portrait of this boy.

'I wish I could have that for my collection at Harvard, Massachusetts,' I murmured. She looked at me quickly.

'It has been against the wall of the closet for years and years,' she said. 'There was no room anywhere in which to hang it, and no one ever sees it. I wish so much that it were possible that you could have it.'

I answered that I realized that it belonged to the library, then I dismissed it from my mind. It was, therefore, with emotion that one day I received a letter from the librarian announcing that the Board of Trustees had voted to present the portrait to me for the new picture gallery about to be erected on the grounds of Fruitlands and the Wayside Museums, Incorporated. Needless to say, I was overjoyed at this good piece of news. I hastened over to Westminster and secured the picture. It is one the visitors always stop in front of and think especially interesting.

The following two letters deal with the artist, Deacon Peckham. One from a lady in Groton, dated December 3, 1938, says:

'In regard to your request for information of old-time portrait painters, I can remember my aunt telling us of a portrait painter by the name of Peckham coming to Westminster where we lived. My grandmother had several portraits painted by him which are still in the family.'

In another letter which I received from a Westminster lady, dated July 28, 1937, she says:

'I have been trying to find someone old enough to remember Mr. Peckham, and found an old lady who told me when she went to school in the schoolhouse located next to his house she often went there for water at noon, as there was no water at the schoolhouse at that time. She said he was a medium-sized man, rather stooped, and wore his hair long with the ends curled under. A stern-looking man, and his wife was a very small woman, but both were kind to children. I have been looking through some old papers of the town hoping to find his signature and it seems as though I should, as he was the deacon of the church, and I have always heard him spoken of as Deacon Peckham, and I have quantities of old papers relating to the church and town so will keep on looking. Mr. Peckham was somewhat of a poet and we have a poem he wrote on the occasion of the dedication of the Soldiers' Monument.'

Deacon Robert Peckham was born December 10, 1785. He married Ruth, daughter of Joseph and Ruth (Wolcott) Sawyer of Bolton, Massachusetts. They lived for a time in Northampton and afterwards at Bolton, but came to Westminster in 1820 for a permanent home. He was a self-made painter by trade, developing an unusual skill along lines of portraiture. He was also successful in landscapes. Deacon Peckham died June 29, 1877, close to ninety-two years old, and was buried in the Woodside Cemetery in Westminster, Massachusetts. He painted John Greenleaf Whittier in 1833.

No less interesting is the picture of Charles L. Eaton and his sister by J. Harvey Young. (Page 68.) This was painted in 1848. It is a large and important picture taking in quite a few of the furnishings of a typical drawing-room of that period. The two children stand in the centre of the picture holding hands. Both have light hair, blue eyes, and fair skin. The girl wears a delicate pink dress with trimmings of white lace and white pantalettes. Around the neck and along the edge of the sleeves is fine embroidered muslin. She wears black shoes, laced, and white stockings. A pink frill falls over the shoulders edged with pink fringe. She holds a bright red book in one hand and the other clasps her brother's. There are three rows of puffings on her sleeves. The boy has a dark blue dress on, black shoes, and white stockings; the same style of frill of white muslin edges the neck and sleeves. With his free hand he holds the reins of a toy horse, which is yellowish in color on a wooden base. The carpet is an old-fashioned Brussels variety with symmetrical designs and flowers scattered over it. It is warm in coloring and is a reddish-brown. Behind the children is a grey marble table; or rather, it is a painted wooden table made to look like marble. The toy horse has a dark mane and dark hoofs.

J. Harvey Young was a Salem, Massachusetts, man, born there in 1830. He began by being an itinerant portrait painter, and this picture was painted during that period. It must have been just after the painting of it that he resolved to set to work seriously to study art, and he moved from Salem to Boston that same year. From then on the style of his painting changed. All suggestion of primitiveness left his work. He then became a prominent portrait painter along established lines, and in 1868 he painted portraits of William Warren, the actor, associated with the Tremont Theatre in Boston, Doctor Peabody of Exeter Academy, Mrs. John H. Holmes of Boston, Horace Mann, Edward Everett, and William H. Prescott, the historian, besides many others, including a number of political men whose portraits now hang in the State Department in Washington.

There are two very attractive portraits (pages 69 and 70) of children painted by Jeremiah Harding that have a distinctive French touch to them. Their names are Eliza and Sarah Amanda Bennett. These portraits were presented to the collection by Mr. and Mrs. C. F. Richardson of Brookline, Massachusetts, being family portraits. They were both painted in 1839. Sarah Amanda Bennett is wearing a grey dress with white lace edging. She carries a grey kitten in her arms and around her neck is a string of coral beads, while over the chair is thrown a red scarf, making the picture a symphony of grey and red that harmonizes very well with her pink cheeks and blue eyes. The background is a greyish-brown merging into a pinkish-grey. Eliza Bennett is wearing the same dress. Evidently the artist was one who carried around with him a varied wardrobe, even to the coral beads, but here a difference comes. Eliza has a blue bonnet with pink trimmings hanging on her arm, also a little fancy basket filled with flowers of varied hue. She holds a soft grey scarf with yellow flowers embroidered on it in her other hand. This is very different from the attire in the other portraits of children described in this book, and as has been said before, these two pictures have a distinctly French touch to them, which adds another influence to the collection. Sarah Amanda was born in 1833, and Eliza was born in 1829.

'For some years previous to 1830, there was in this city [Lowell, Massachusetts] a painter named Jeremiah Harding.

He was skillful in many directions and painted not only signs, banners, and ornamental work generally, but also portraits with more or less success.' This was copied from *Vox Populi*, Lowell, December, 1877.

A portrait (page 71) from Hancock, New Hampshire, by H. Bundy, 1850, portrays another of those anemic-looking children in a white embroidered muslin dress. Her hair is light and she has blue eyes, and sits on a bright red cushion. Her little feet are bare, and her hands are playing with them. The background is yellowish-grey with a dark oval line enclosing the picture. Bundy wandered far afield in New England. He was painting in Springfield, Vermont, in 1808, and at Hancock, New Hampshire, in 1850, when he painted this portrait. It is supposed to be the only one of a child that he painted. He also painted a portrait of Governor Steele about that time, and others as well, for I received a letter from a gentleman in Dedham, Massachusetts, mentioning two family portraits of his in oil by H. Bundy, which he painted in Claremont, New Hampshire, in 1846, 'which have been much admired by those in a position to know of the art of that day.'

Quite a unique child's portrait (page 72) is one of Henry Munro and his twin brother, painted by Ferdinand T. L. Boyle in 1850. The baby twins have little almost hairless heads. The varnish in years had turned to an orange yellow when I found it, which made them look like newly hatched chickens, and I called them the 'Easter eggs.' When the varnish was removed the flesh tints came out delicate and lovely. One little boy has his arm around his brother's shoulder and is pointing to a crumpled butterfly lying prostrate on the table on which they lean. The two figures are enclosed in an oval, the background of which is dark, the rest of the square canvas being of a greyish-yellow.

Boyle came of English parentage. He was born in 1820. He was brought to this country as a child, and when he grew to be a youth he tried to make his way as a painter starting on the open road, and had the good fortune finally to study under Inman. He became quite a notable person. In 1855, five years after he painted the portrait of the twins, he went to St. Louis and organized the Western Academy of Art. After ten years he came to New York, and there he painted a number of celebrities, including Charles Dickens, Archbishop Hughes, General Grant, Edgar Allan Poe, and others. Then for many years he was a professor at the Brooklyn Institute of Art. He died in 1906. He had pushed his way to the front very successfully.

One fascinating portrait (page 73) is of a little girl in a full-skirted white dress edged with a line of bright blue stitching. Her pantalettes are white, edged with lace tatting, some of which is also on the sleeves. The white bodice is smocked, and on it are small spots of bright blue. Blue edges the neck also and follows in two rows down the sleeves of the dress. The child's hair is bright red and her eyes are blue. She wears a string of coral beads around her neck and a fine narrow gold bracelet around her wrist. Her little hand is holding a full-blown moss rose.

One small red curl, like a half-moon, lies on the girl's forehead. There is a landscape in part of the background which one sees through an open window, on the sill of which is a plant abloom with pink flowers and green leaves. The rest is dark maroon with red curtains on either side. The little girl sits on a stool covered with a carpet of fancy-colored design; the floor is grey, striped with yellow brown, the lines of which are an inch wide. She has on white stockings and amazing little brown shoes. One cannot get away from this portrait. The arch expression on the child's face is so sweet yet so challenging one wonders what she was like when she grew up to womanhood. Unfortunately, the artist did not sign his name to the portrait. It is a great pity.

I considered it a find when I came across the portrait (page 74) of a little girl whose full blue dress hung over a large hoop skirt. There was no artist's name signed to it, but whoever painted it certainly knew how to make an attractive portrait of a child of that period. She is standing flat-footed upon the ground. Her white pantalettes are as stiff as cardboard, edged with lace. She is a plump little thing and clutches a bunch of small red and white roses with both hands, but the thing above all others that makes one smile is the look of determination written all over her little face. She has such great big blue eyes and pretty brown hair. Behind her as a background is a wood scene. The old-fashioned expression 'cute' fits her perfectly It is quite certain she would have her own way through life.

There is another unsigned portrait of three children which is very decorative and full of color. (Page 75.) The combination is one girl and two boys. The girl wears a red dress, low in the neck and with short sleeves. The older boy wears a bright blue dress with pantalettes which also is low in the neck and with short sleeves. The baby has an orange-colored dress. It is also low in the neck with short sleeves. The girl holds a pink rose in her hand, and the oldest boy a toy whip. The portrait comes from Massachusetts, but from which town has not as yet been ascertained. That discovery may turn up at any time, however. This picture demonstrates what has been said before in regard to the custom of dressing small boys like girls up to a certain age.

I must not leave out a description of the portrait of Aloyishus Brown (page 76) also unsigned, because it satisfactorily demonstrates the theory that it is the atmosphere that goes out from a picture that counts, rather than its technical makeup; for Aloyishus stands rather uncertainly upon his baby feet, and in spite of his woodeny and thick-set structure, there is an awkward twist and turn to the little body that is exceedingly characteristic of a child of that age. While the artist's name is not attached to the portrait, I personally am of the opinion that it was painted by Joseph M. Stock of Springfield. He was painting a great deal at the time that Elwell was painting, and he seems to have made a specialty of children. He had one peculiarity that was very noticeable, which was that the heads were always too big for the bodies, and were very square on top. I have seen one portrait of his of a small boy named Wilbur Gorham, a brother of the William Henry Gorham who was painted by Elwell. He painted the head of this child so square that I am convinced a plate could have rested securely upon it without any danger of breakage. And yet the rest of the portrait was well done.

Stock was born in Springfield, Massachusetts, in 1815, and died in 1855. He was very much hampered in his career because he was crippled and could not get about except in a wheel-chair. His career as an artist did not last for very long. He was finally obliged to satisfy himself by having a studio in Springfield, and from there he sent out advertisements. In 1846 he went into partnership with a man by the name of Cooley, and the following advertisement appeared in a local paper:

'Likenesses taken in a superior manner ... in groups from two to seven persons. A perfect and satisfactory likeness guaranteed.... Portraits from eight dollars to twenty-five dollars.'

To go back to Aloyishus. He has light hair and blue eyes, his dress is of a reddish-brown color striped with black and green. His pantalettes are white and his shoes brown. There is an embroidered frill around his short sleeves and low-cut neck. He leans against a black haircloth and mahogany chair. A red curtain forms a part of the background. The rest is very dark brown and somewhat shaded. In his right hand the boy holds a bright red apple.

CHAPTER IV

H AVE you ever been to Hollis, New Hampshire? If not, you have missed something. Lovely old New England homes are dotted on either side of the road that runs through the village, their fronts shaded by a row of grand old maple trees interspersed with towering elms that give a sort of homelike, genial look to the place as though it were a centre of good neighbors, while the backs of these houses look out across green pastures and rolling uplands and here and there patches of deep woods. One has a curious sensation of friendly intercourse mixed with great solitude. It is all pure New England.

I received a letter from a dear old lady who lived in one of these houses telling me that she had a portrait painted by an itinerant artist named Roswell T. Smith. It was a family portrait and she was very anxious that I should see it, so one day shortly after that I motored over to Hollis. I found the lady at home and she gave me a cordial welcome, characteristic of the old houses, and asked me to sit down while she went upstairs to get the picture.

While she was gone I sat enjoying the quiet of the place. It was a day in August, and I could hear sounds from the near-by farms, distant lowing of cattle, barking of a dog in a neighboring yard, every now and then the calling of crows as they quarrelled in a grove of evergreens. It seemed as if the world had suddenly come to a standstill, and I was quite startled when my hostess came in bearing the picture of a young girl with strangely speaking eyes and a delicate thoughtful face. (Page 93.) Her name was Lucy Ober. I asked the lady if she could tell me anything about the artist who had painted the portrait, and she said she had always heard of him as R. T. Smith. (It was not until later that I discovered his name was Roswell.) She had heard her father speak of him frequently, and he painted very many portraits there and in neighboring towns. She remembered he told her that the boys, not knowing what his initials, R. T., stood for, gave him the nickname of 'Rat Tail Smith.' When his wagon came along the road filled with canvases ready for a day's work, they used to call out 'Here comes Rat Tail,' little realizing the tragedy that was shadowing his life; for both his legs were practically withered, one more than the other, and he could not follow the open road on foot as so many of the itinerant portrait painters did. He was, so to speak, chained to his crutches. When he stopped at a farmhouse to suggest to the inmates that they might want to have their portraits painted, all the people in the near-by houses looked out of their windows or came out of their front doors to look down the road where his wagon was, and watched him make the painful descent to the ground, fearing every moment that he might fall and give himself further injury.

Smith was a young man. They say he had a very noticeable face, clear features and a handsome brow, and he asked help from nobody; in fact, he resented it if one of the kindly neighbors offered to assist him. His trouble all dated back to the time when at four years old he was chased by some pigs; after running on his little feet as fast as he could, he fell and was so badly injured that his legs were ruined for life. As he grew up his father, who was a learned man, took in some students to board, and as the village school was some distance away from his father's farm, he could not join the other boys and scholars, so these students were very kind to him and he learned a great deal from them. As time went on, the teacher of the school took him in hand and taught him things that he would not otherwise have had the opportunity of learning. He was a

PORTRAIT OF LUCY OBER OF HOLLIS, NEW HAMPSHIRE
Painted by Roswell T. Smith of Nashua in 1858.
(Description, page 91)

PORTRAIT OF CHARLES M. HODGE
Painted by Lorenzo Somerby, Boston, Massachusetts, in 1838.
(Description, page 110)

PORTRAIT OF ELIZABETH DAVENPORT OF MENDON, MASSACHUSETTS
(LATER MRS. JONATHAN DODGE WHEELER)
Artist unknown. Painted in 1829.
(Description, page 110)

PORTRAIT OF JONATHAN DODGE WHEELER OF GRAFTON,
MASSACHUSETTS
Artist unknown. Painted in 1829.
(Description, page 110)

PORTRAIT OF A WOMAN FROM MARBLEHEAD, MASSACHUSETTS
Artist unknown.
(Description, page 113)

PORTRAIT OF MISS SUSAN P. LIVERMORE OF MELROSE,
MASSACHUSETTS
Painted by Isaac A. Wetherbee in 1840.
(Description, page 114)

PORTRAIT OF MR. BENT, PROPRIETOR OF THE OLD NEW IPSWICH
INN, NEW IPSWICH, NEW HAMPSHIRE
Artist unknown. Painted in 1843.
(Description, pages 114, 115)

PORTRAIT OF AN OLD NEW ENGLAND WOMAN OF MASSACHUSETTS
Artist unknown. Painted about 1848.
(Description, page 115)

very able pupil, and seemed to absorb knowledge from all directions. He occupied his leisure hours making fans, which he peddled about amongst the neighbors.

Perhaps, being as incapacitated as he was, Smith had more time for reflection than other boys. He studied nature, and grew to realize that he had a longing to express the sense of beauty which he felt stirring within him. His father could not make any use of him on the farm, and the boy began to occupy himself with palette and paint brush, and finally insisted upon trying his luck as a portrait painter. The only way to accomplish anything in that line was to go out and seek the work, so his father let him have an old wagon and an old horse, and one day he started forth on his new venture.

It was hard work at first. Roswell was young, and people did not take him seriously. Besides, his poor legs occupied so much of their attention that they could hardly consider him in the light of an artist, who they thought should be a man with all his physical being intact; but he persisted, and it was not long before he began to have a good many orders. Without any instruction whatsoever he relied upon the talent which he felt was growing within him all the time, and he gave his instincts full play. He got to be so familiar an object in his wagon that the time came when he arrived in the village that the boys called out 'Rat Tail Smith' in a different tone of voice from what they had used in the beginning. There was almost a note of affection in it, for he was always pleasant with them, and took their fun good-naturedly.

I watched the picture carefully as the old lady was telling me about the young artist. It showed a good deal of imagination and a good sense of drawing. It was the expression of the face that struck me as unusual. The eyes were what you might call 'seeing eyes.'

It was very pleasant sitting there and hearing the description of long-gone days, so different from our modern ones, and the little old lady was so kindly that it produced in me a feel-

ing of calm and confidence. I was very much touched therefore when suddenly she turned to me and said, 'I have no one
to leave this picture to, but I want it to be preserved, and I
have heard of your collection and the picture gallery you are
planning to build, and now I am offering it to you as a gift if
you will accept it.' It was all so simply said and there was
something so genuine about it that I felt quite overcome. I
said, indeed I should be very glad and honored to have it take
its place in the new picture gallery, and thanked her with real
sincerity of heart, especially as I was a total stranger to her.

We then talked more about R. T. Smith, and I asked her
what 'R. T.' stood for. She said she could not remember, but
there was an old lady who lived farther up the road who could
tell me more about him, and I had better go and see her, so I
went up the road and found another old house, where I
knocked on the door. The lady that let me in there was a
bright and shining example of what one could be at ninety-
four years. Her eyes were bright and full of intelligence, and
though she was somewhat decrepit, I did not think of it, because she was so cordial and so spontaneous in greeting me.

I told her the errand I was on.

'R. T. Smith?' she said. 'Why, his name was Roswell —
Roswell T. Smith. Well I remember him'; and she repeated
all that the other old lady had told me. Then she said, 'You
know, there are other portraits in town by Roswell T. Smith;
two of them are owned by a lady who lives in a house along
the road on the right-hand side about a quarter of a mile from
here.'

Before going I got her to tell me something about herself,
and I found that, though she was tucked away in this old New
England town, when she was very young she had wandered
far afield and was a schoolteacher in Nebraska and later in
Chicago for thirty-nine years. But before that she had worked
in the little bookstore which after his itinerant days were
over Roswell T. Smith started in Nashua, New Hampshire.

That bookstore has left many memories behind it, because it became the meeting place of all of the lovers of books in that vicinity, and if there are tales of the interesting days of the Old Corner Book Store in Boston, Roswell T. Smith's little bookstore vied with it in interest in a humble way among the people of Nashua, who congregated there and talked over the latest books, and discussed their merits; it gave a literary turn to what was becoming a mill town.

But to go back to Smith's itinerant days. I followed along the road according to this lady's directions and arrived at a lovely old house with brick ends and knocked at the door. Her friend who let me in was very gracious, and I told her my errand and she said, 'Oh, yes; my father remembered Mr. Smith very well and admired him greatly,' and then she began to tell me more about the artist, and led me into the dining-room, where over the mantel was the loveliest old portrait of her grandmother painted by him. I was amazed that anyone far up country whose life had been so restricted could have painted a portrait like that. It was very decidedly under the Dutch influence. After looking at it, I turned to her and said, 'Why, it might be a Holbein,' and she said, 'Many have said it was suggestive of Vermeer.' And really it was.

I secretly wished that this portrait could have been in my collection, but, of course, I knew that was impossible. It was a very much prized family portrait, and no wonder. I include a small description of it in order to demonstrate some of the work of this interesting painter.

The lady in the portrait was sitting facing her public in a dark red chair. Her dress was of heavy black silk. Around her throat was a delicate lace collar caught together with an old-fashioned breastpin. On her grey hair was a little white cap with ties which were knotted under her chin. The red curtain which formed a part of the background was drawn aside enough to show a glimpse of Wachusett Mountain. From out of this picture gleamed a pair of deeply intelligent eyes set in a charming smiling face. The effect it produced on one was warm and genial. It was as if you were conversing with a person of keen understanding.

Apparently Roswell T. Smith felt that this was his best piece of work, for sometime after painting it, so my hostess said, quoting her father, he stood looking at it and remarked thoughtfully, 'Well, that is a good piece of work, even if I do say so.'

When we had examined the portrait sufficiently, my hostess said, 'I have another portrait to show you by Roswell T. Smith,' and she brought forth one of a young woman painted in a grey dress with dainty white cuffs on her sleeves, and a pink necktie wound around her throat and tied in a little bow under her chin. Her arms were folded. She had a pleasing face — even pretty — but the picture did not compare with that of the old lady.

'He was in love with her,' said my hostess in a very low tone, with almost a tinge of awe in it. 'That is why it is not as good as the other; he was too nervous and agitated. He suffered a great deal thinking of his infirmities. He hardly dared to hope for her love in return, but he could not hide his feelings from her.' The longer he took to paint the portrait, the more his emotions grew, and finally one day he told her what was troubling him. She did not answer at first. There had been so much charm in sitting there watching his handsome profile, as he bent his head and then raised it, his eyes meeting hers with a look in them she could not mistake. She could not bring herself to refuse him, and yet she could not bring herself to accept him. She was in a quandary of doubt. As she thought it over, she hardly had the courage to marry a man so handicapped, and so physically unable to do his share in the work of life.

For a time, they were two very unhappy young people. When the portrait was finished, however, she had made up her mind. It could not be. She told him frankly how she felt

about it. There was nothing for him to say. He was too conscientious to urge her, knowing that her decision was the
right one, and so they parted. She watched him from her
window as he drove his old wagon down the road with a
feeling of numbness around her heart. The pleasant days were
over. He was driving away out of her life.

I received a letter from a lady in Nashua, and she speaks of
an episode in Roswell T. Smith's life that must have come
some little time after this one, for we find him in Pepperell,
Massachusetts, painting other portraits. It appears there was
a gentleman named Marshall there who owned a certain number of houses, and he entered into communication with Smith,
as he wanted a portrait painted of his daughter, and wished
him to do the work. So Smith went to Mr. Marshall's home,
a fine old house nestling under the thick branches of maple
trees, and there he met the young girl whose portrait he was
to paint. She was very sweet and lovely, and he was young,
and being an artist by nature he found himself again falling in
love. All the mixed feelings of joy and emotion and appre-
hension and distress began surging through him again, but
this time the girl responded to his love in spite of his infirmities, and in spite of his being incapacitated from doing his
share of the work of life.

His love of beauty and his natural artistic temperament,
and his keen interest in so many of the things he saw about
him, made a tremendous appeal to her, but unfortunately for
him, her father objected to the match. 'I cannot have my
daughter marrying a man without legs,' he said, and she, being a high-spirited girl, replied, 'But I would rather marry a
man without legs but with a brain than a man with legs and
no brain!' But in those days a parent's consent was a necessity, and Roswell T. Smith drove away in his old wagon for
the second time with a heavy heart and a feeling of intense
discouragement.

The lady who wrote me these details added in her letter,

'This story was always told as a fact by members of the family.' In another letter, she writes:

'I am glad that someone has given you an account of Mr. Smith's portrait painting.... Both of Mr. Smith's legs were affected. One, however, was nearly normal in size. He swung his body between two crutches. He always wore a long military cape and beneath it a Prince Albert cut unusually long. When climbing stairs or entering or leaving a carriage he used to put both crutches under his left arm, and used his right to raise or lower himself. His arms were very strong, and his hands were as beautiful as Henry van Dyke's. Mr. Smith was a great student. He read a great deal and was very fond of Emerson. He wrote well, and some of his poems were very fine. He always published them anonymously. I think I may be able to find one or two of them if you care to have them.

'As time went on,' she continued, 'he was religious but not pious. He was always interested in young people, and they adored him, and frequently sought his advice.'

In trying to follow Smith's career we find him next in Nashua, New Hampshire. Some years have passed. He was very much discouraged by his two romances and their outcome. A feeling almost of resentment was stealing over him to find himself deprived of so much that would make life seem worth living, and now it appears that his health began to fail, and he had no one to take care of him or to help him.

One day his old schoolmistress turned up, and seeing how things were with her old pupil she began to see what she could do to help him. She was a warm-hearted and capable New England woman, but all she could say or do did not seem to bring back any of the joy of life to him. Finally, an occasion came when she said something that startled him.

'You ought to be married,' she said. 'You ought to have a wife to see that you are made comfortable and to cook your meals and to do all the things for you that any decent-hearted woman would be only too glad to do.'

He looked up at her in complete surprise. 'No woman would think of me as a husband,' he replied. 'I have had my experience along that line.'

'Just the same,' she said, 'you ought to be married.'

'Who will marry me?' he asked. 'Who will undertake to marry a man crippled as I am?'

'I will,' she answered, 'and I am going to do it right away. You have gone long enough without anyone to look after you.'

And so, in spite of the difference in age, they were married. It was a strange situation, but Mrs. Smith carried it off with flying colors. She was a forceful, motherly woman, and by her persistent care she brought his health back and his courage back. Though she turned her face against his continuing to be an itinerant portrait painter, knowing the energy of his mental makeup and his keen enthusiasm for work, she it was who suggested opening the little bookstore which proved such an inspiring meeting place to the booklovers of Nashua.

The lady who wrote me before gave another short account of him. She could just remember him when she was a child.

'When sitting in his big chair in the bay window of his living-room,' she wrote, 'his legs were always covered with an afghan or a linen robe or duster, such as was used in a carriage. He was always well groomed. I had always wished that someone had painted his portrait as he sat in his favorite place with his fine profile so clearly defined in the strong light. His shoulders were broad, and his chest deep. His bookstore was also an art centre. I do not remember when he conducted this bookstore. He finally sold it to two of his cousins. I think he was always interested in it.... Stretching canvases and framing were two services rendered by the firm.'

Now it happened that this unusual couple began to feel the want of a child about the house to add to their happiness, and they adopted a little boy and brought him up to manhood. During the passing years Smith's attention seemed to turn towards inventions, and it goes to show how a man of talent, in whatever channel it reveals itself, can change and turn about if the chosen avenue is closed, and all the inventive power within him can flow down in other directions.

Few know now that the player-piano was one of Roswell T. Smith's inventions, or the lace-making machine, which proved to be very popular. Other inventions of his were:

> Power shearing machine.
> Flexible cable for power.
> Cloth-cutting machine for bags.
> Music perforators.
> Bag folder and cutter.
> Automatic machine for embroidery.
> Power embroidery machine (which was sold to Germany).
> Machine for folding fans (this started well but was ruined by importations from Japan).
> Gang circular saw.
> Multiple die.
> Machine for pasting two webs of cloth together.
> Cloth-trimming machine.
> Butt-hinge riveting machine.
> Lace-making machine (sold to Germany).
> Change purse. (This invention was never registered, and Mr. Smith gave out the work to veterans of the Civil War. He had a big demand for the purses.)

This will show what a talented man Smith was, and that though crippled, he never allowed his life to be ruined by his infirmities.

The lady who wrote all this to me told me that there was an old gentleman of eighty-three years who had imparted the following bit of information: that in his early days Roswell T. Smith always lived in upstairs tenements, so as to avoid shovelling snow.

From here on, Roswell T. Smith became exceedingly interested in town affairs, and became literally one of the town fathers, but with all these various activities and all the shifting scenes in his life, according to my first informant, he never forgot his first love. Whenever he found anyone going to Hollis, upon their return he would say to them, 'Is all well with Miss X?' and when they said all was well, he turned and talked of other things. Apparently his wife took note of this and began to resent it, and if there was any question of their meeting again she so arranged it that the plan was frustrated. Perhaps that was natural, anyway it was very womanlike, and though she was so much his senior, and married him just to take care of him, she evidently did not want the past to dim the brightness of their present day. So there is the tale of Roswell T. Smith, itinerant portrait painter.

One very curious thing about it is that after he married the schoolteacher no one in his family ever referred to his itinerant days as a portrait painter, and when he died a long obituary notice was written of him in the leading newspaper of Nashua, but of his earlier days and the many portraits that he had painted all through that section of the state, no mention was made. Yet that was the romantic period of his life which he never forgot, in spite of the happy and comfortable years which followed them. He was a devoted husband, and the schoolteacher made a devoted wife.

There were undoubtedly many romances in those days between artists and sitters which never will come to the surface, but I did receive a short account of another by a gentleman from Newbury, Massachusetts, of an artist by the name of Lorenzo Somerby, who painted a great many portraits around Salem and Newburyport and all other coast towns. I was especially interested in this because there is one of his portraits in the collection at Harvard, Massachusetts. I quote from the letter I received:

'I have in my attic a portrait of Matilda Plummer painted by Somerby in 1838, as written on the back. The story as told me by my ancestors, now passed on, is that Somerby was in

love with Matilda, and had painted a picture for her, which I
also have, and then persuaded her to allow him to paint her
portrait, upon the completion of which he proposed marriage,
but was, as the old saying went, "given the mitten." '

The portrait by Somerby at Harvard is that of a young man,
and is signed 'Lorenzo Somerby, Boston, January 9, 1838.'
It is a portrait of Charles M. Hodge, and is painted on a
wooden panel. (Page 94.) The young man has a thoughtful
and romantic face, which, taken as a whole, is a very charming one, and sympathetically painted.

These accounts show that in spite of the drudgery and
labors of the old-time itinerant artists, Cupid insisted upon
being let in, to have a finger in the pie.

Somerby was born on August 9, 1816, at Newburyport,
Massachusetts. Where he died is still uncertain.

Another quite romantic find I made in 1938 was when I received a letter from a lady in Fitchburg, who asked me to
come to see two portraits which she had inherited, but for
which she had no room in the smaller house into which she
and her husband were moving. The account which she gave
rather interested me, so I went to see her. I found that she
had not overpraised the portraits when writing to me. They
are certainly especially well painted and very interesting. One
(page 95) is of Elizabeth Davenport of Mendon, Massachusetts, a young girl in a dove-colored dress with lustrous
brown hair piled high on top of her head, and twisted into
innumerable curls and puffs, a structure that must have taken
a long time to build up. She had a rather delicate face with
great brown eyes, and it was not surprising that Jonathan
Dodge Wheeler of Brockton, Massachusetts, fell very deeply
in love with her. His portrait (page 96) depicts a very good-
looking young man, and it is not surprising either that she
fell in love with him. Both portraits are very striking.

Elizabeth and Jonathan each came from families that were
very prominent in the towns from which they came. What

brings them into intimate touch with this day and age is that a little trunk was found in the attic of the house where the portraits were, containing the love letters of these two young people. They are very different from the love letters of these days. Elizabeth's begin 'Dear Jonathan' and many of them end 'Your friend Elizabeth Davenport.' Pages of them are written on the advisability of being careful in the winter weather so as not to catch cold. Elizabeth writes, 'Be sure, Jonathan, that you wear your overcoat, and take care of yourself,' and sometimes she reproaches him a little for being a bit too fond of the things of this world. There is a faint suggestion in Jonathan's eyes that might bear out her statement, and he has very handsome eyes. But he was devoted to Elizabeth, and he in his turn wrote reams on the subject of the care she should take of herself in the rigorous winter weather. A visit to Boston furnished more pages from her to him. She told him of the sights she had seen and of the relatives she had visited, while he at the other end waited impatiently for her return.

If Jonathan did not go to see her whenever the opportunity presented itself, Elizabeth would write demurely that she hoped he did not mean that he did not care to come, but she had looked for him. And if she did not write to him almost every day, he in his turn questioned as to whether she was thinking about him as much as she ought to. This went on for letter after letter and apparently was the extent of their love-making; on one occasion she wrote to him that he must understand that she could not think of marrying a man of whom her family and all her friends did not approve. She admitted that they did approve of him, which was quite understandable, as he certainly was very attractive in appearance.

I was fortunate in being able to acquire this little trunk of love letters with the portraits, and having read them all, I feel when I look at the faces of Jonathan and Elizabeth that I have had a glimpse into their hearts, and therefore know them intimately, which adds much to my pleasure.

Poor little Elizabeth Davenport, who seemed to be troubled with conscientious scruples such as no girl would feel in these days, was not destined to have a long life, for she died a year after her marriage. In the small trunk I found a pathetic little bundle. Opening it with great care, I found a purse inside and a paper yellow with age wrapped around it. The ink was already fading which the young husband had used to write the following line: 'This was my beloved's purse as she left it. I shall follow her soon.'

But that is something that man cannot decide. Jonathan was very young and full of life, and it was not long before he chose another wife; in 1834 he married Caroline A. Norcross, daughter of Otis Norcross, Esq., and sister of Otis Norcross, Jr., who was once mayor of Boston. This lady was of a completely different temperament from his first love, who always reminded me of Dora in Charles Dickens's *David Copperfield*. Jonathan now began his life as a sober business man and became the owner of Wheeler's Cotton Mill at Millbury, Massachusetts; this was a very successful venture, and many others followed.

These two portraits were painted in 1829 by some unknown artist.

I will, however, include a letter on this subject. On January 29, 1940, I received a letter from a gentleman, who wrote as follows:

'An article in today's *Worcester Sunday Telegram* showing a picture of an oil painting of Elizabeth Davenport (later Mrs. Jonathan Dodge Wheeler) of Mendon, Massachusetts, caught my eye as bearing a striking resemblance in some respects to an oil painting in my possession. My painting is of one of my ancestors, probably a great-aunt.

'I know nothing about portraits or their painters, but the pose of the head, the eyes and nose, shape of the head, and slope of the shoulders bear a very striking resemblance to the painting I have.

'My painting was done by an Ebenezer Baker White, my grandfather's brother. He was born in Sutton, or North-bridge, Massachusetts, on February 16, 1806, lived in Smith-field, Rhode Island (just over the Massachusetts line), and Providence. He was alive in 1849 or 1841. My ancestors came to Mendon from Weymouth, Massachusetts, and lived in Uxbridge, Northbridge, and Sutton. One genealogy mentions this Ebenezer White as "he resided in Providence, Rhode Island, where he became a portrait painter of some note."

'Yours very truly,

'(Signed) ——'

Romance is still to the fore. I will describe a portrait (page 97) which is in the collection that comes from Marblehead. It is of a very good-looking young woman in a black satin dress with a broad muslin kerchief over her shoulders and a fascinating muslin cap on her head. She has clear-cut features and a beautiful skin. It might be a portrait of Priscilla Alden from the way she is dressed, but an interesting point about her portrait is that it had been shot through the heart by somebody, no one knows who. One could write a romance on such a theme. Was it revenge meted out after she was dead and gone? Or disappointed love? Or was it just mischievous boys at play in the garret? No one can tell now.

The portrait dates back to the time when Marblehead was a strange and unique place in which to live. The people were of a very rough kind, and kept entirely to themselves. My mother, who was born in Salem, used to tell me that she and her sisters were fond of riding horseback, but were told never to go near Marblehead, as the inhabitants resented the approach of strangers. There were all kinds of tales about those who intruded upon the inhabitants.

One day one of my aunts, being young and venturesome, rode over there and penetrated into one of the streets. Stones were thrown at her and other missiles! Fortunately, she was riding a good horse and she galloped away as fast as she could and was glad to get back safely to her home in Salem. She never attempted to go again. It is hard to believe all this when you see Marblehead of today filled with tourists!

The name of the artist who painted this picture is, as yet, unknown.

When I came upon the portrait (page 98) of Miss Susan P. Livermore of Melrose, Massachusetts, painted by Isaac A. Wetherbee in 1840, I simply could not resist her. I had never seen anyone with such a long throat before, and I looked upon it as sort of a freak of nature, until an artist in speaking of it said, 'The throat is in correct measurements with the breadth of the eyes, and therefore is not out of drawing,' and he found so much to admire in the portrait that I began to look upon it differently. He drew attention to the admirable way in which the lace collar was painted, showing the neck through, and the quiet serenity of the pose, the calm of the brow, and the pleasant expression of the countenance.

Say what you will, I still think the neck is appallingly long, but I try to see from his point that it might have been so by nature. And, strange to say, I have grown quite fond of the portrait.

A very quaint portrait that hung for many years on the walls of the old inn at New Ipswich, New Hampshire, is that of Mr. Bent (page 99), the long-ago proprietor. His was a very famous hostelry in its day, and from his looks one can readily see that he was the true type of an old-fashioned landlord.

Mr. Bent married a Miss Appleton of Boston, and I had the curious experience when the portrait was hanging on the wall of the Trustees' Room at Fruitlands and the Wayside Museums, Incorporated, to have one of a party of ladies upon entering the room exclaim: 'Why, there is grandfather's portrait! How did you come by it?' This was a well-known Boston woman, and another time a party of ladies was entering the room for the first time and one of them exclaimed, 'Why, there is grandfather's portrait!' I began to think that a whole family would be landed upon me, and that one relative would bring out many more to see it.

It appears that Grandfather Bent was a gentleman of genial habits, a little too genial for the comfort of his family; therefore, when he died his portrait was left hanging on the walls of the old New Ipswich Inn, and there it hung until I procured it through a friend. I think if you will look at Grandfather Bent's face, you will see that he took life easily, and one might even suggest merrily. Unfortunately, as usual, the artist did not sign his name.

The portrait (page 100), 'An Old New England Woman,' makes a strong appeal to many who see it. The woman's face tells so many things. The brow is so calm, but it is the calm of self-control, of patient waiting, of resignation. The square chin denotes strength of character. The expression in the eyes suggests long years of upright living. There is a dignity to the simple pose of the body and the unconscious, unassuming, but self-respecting lift of the head. I have known many like her in the old New England villages. She is just the type that inspires her sons and daughters who have left the old home and gone to the cities to say at Thanksgiving time: 'We're going back home to the farm today. We want to see Mother.'

The portrait is not signed. It was evidently painted about 1848.

CHAPTER V

Painting in oils was not the only medium used by the itinerant portrait painters for expressing their art. Pastels were also very popular, and there were certain artists who made a name for themselves by adopting that style of painting. The softness of the coloring appealed to many. Moreover, they were done in a very sketchy way, leaving a good deal to the imagination in regard to detail, but producing a very illusive and often flattering effect. These artists were kinder to their sitters than were the painters in oil. Truth was the battle-cry of these last. If a lady was so unfortunate as to have a mole on her forehead, or a man so afflicted as to have a wart on his nose, they were targets for persecution. Not one jot or tittle of those disfigurements was left unrecorded. On the contrary, the artists seemed to paint them with the utmost care. There is one oil portrait in the Fruitlands collection that exemplifies this dramatically. It is a portrait of a lady wearing a wonderfully embroidered cap; not only are several unsightly blemishes carefully reproduced, but her tendency to have a dark mustache is not allowed to escape notice, and boldly challenges any protests on the part of those viewing the picture. Perhaps in those days people were proud of such defects. I once knew of an old lady in the country who would not have parted with her unsightly wart for any money on earth, because her great-grandfather had worn one like it all through his old age. To her mind, therefore, it was a mark of distinction.

You see, one has to be careful in the judging of these things.

There are two pastels in the Fruitlands collection which are very interesting. (Pages 133 and 134.) They are the portraits of Elias Trafton of Swansea, Massachusetts, and his wife Sophronia Perry Trafton, painted in the year of their marriage in 1820. Sophronia Perry Trafton was the sister of the famous Commodore Perry.

These portraits are not signed, but an incident occurred in my wanderings which made it beyond question that they were painted by Doyle, for I came across another couple done in pastels that were posed and dressed and painted in exactly the same style, with hair done in identically the same fashion, and this fashion was a peculiar one, as the hair was banged and spread over the forehead in ropes, a style the Emperor Napoleon adopted at the time of the First Empire. Both costumes were of that period. These portraits were signed by Doyle. They belonged to a lady who had inherited them, and were of her great-grandparents. She valued them as precious heritages of the past. I will say, however, that I think those in the Fruitlands collection are more carefully painted than hers, and though the former are not signed, their historic value is greater.

The portrait of Elias Trafton shows a rather stout man with dark brown hair brushed to the front and in long stringy bangs around the forehead. He wears a black coat and high white collar wrapped around with a stock. The vest is white.

Sophronia Perry Trafton has a white dress, with the waistline directly under the bust. Her hair is brown and built into a big knot on top of her head, and she wears a bang around her forehead similar to that of her husband. A black velvet ribbon is tied around her head; in her ears are red pendant earrings, and a small necklace of beads of the same color hangs around her neck. The sleeves of the dress are short with long tight undersleeves emerging from them, coming close to the wrist. Both these portraits are painted with great care as to effect and detail.

As we are on the subject of pastels, I do not think any work about the early painters could possibly omit the name of Ruth Henshaw, better known by her married name, Bascom; for not only was she very much sought after for pastels in her part of the country, but also she was a very picturesque character. I have received a great many letters asking if one of her portraits was in the collection at Fruitlands and the Wayside Museums, Incorporated; I have had to admit that there were none, but I am certainly hoping that some day I may be able to procure one.

I received a letter dated January 9, 1939, from two very delightful and interesting sisters living in Leicester, Massachusetts. In it one of them says:

'A friend spoke to me recently about your request for information about Ruth Henshaw Bascom, who made pastel portraits three or four generations ago. Perhaps you have already found out what you wanted to know, but if not, I think my sister and I may be able to help you and will be very glad to do so, for we have some of her portraits and more important still her diaries kept during the last part of her life. She was a great-aunt, and we have a good deal of manuscript material about the family.'

The following February 23 I received another letter:

'My sister and I hope what we are sending you will be what you wanted to know about Ruth (Henshaw) Bascom. My sister has at various times during past years patiently copied (with the aid of a reading glass) extracts from the diaries with their very difficult chirography. If this helps to bring to life one of the old-time artists we shall be very glad, though I am afraid you may be disappointed that there is so little about her work as an artist.'

Ruth Henshaw was born December 15, 1772, the eldest of ten children of Colonel William Henshaw and his wife, Phoebe Swan. Her father was a direct descendant of Thomas Henshaw of Toxter Park, England (died there in 1630). A very romantic story is attached to the coming of two Henshaw brothers, his grandsons, to this country in 1653. Suffice it to say that the Henshaws trace their descent from a royal family of England. Colonel William, Ruth's father, served during two campaigns of the French and Indian Wars, and was appointed adjutant general at the time of the Revolution, serving in that capacity until the arrival at Cambridge of General Gates, whose assistant he then became. It was on his motion before the Provincial Congress that the companies of 'Minute Men' were authorized to be formed in the various towns.

Colonel William's mother was Elizabeth Alden, daughter of John and Priscilla. Ruth's childhood was spent in the Henshaw home on what is now Reservoir Street, Worcester, Massachusetts, a farm deeded to her great-grandfather as one of the original proprietors of Worcester. He himself never lived there, as he was a Boston merchant.

When she was seventeen years old, Ruth began the diaries which she kept for fifty-seven years, and which consist largely of brief jottings from day to day, never enlarging upon facts. But they give an excellent idea of the home life of that time, and so a few quotations may be of interest.

'Went to town and dined at Uncle Swan's with Cousin Moses Richardson. Drank tea at Mr. Scott's, then returned to Uncle Swan's in the evening. Spent a very agreeable evening with girl friends. Played book games, "Nick the Weaver," "Grind the Salt," danced some, sang songs, etc. We stayed all night.'

'Quilting at Mr. Andrews'. Had a great number of gallants. "Wool break" at Mr. Southgate's, spinning frolic at Mr. Green's. Had a Cappadocian Dance. Mr. Shaw played for us.'

'Betsy and I carding and spinning. Later we went to pick blackberries out of Old Mrs. Andrews' pasture and she was mad as hops.'

[119]

'Spun and sang songs all day until night approached.'

'A dancing school held at Landlord Waite's. We learned "Freedom" and "Assembly" steps. The master had us practice upon "New Jersey," "King's Return," and "Belles of New York." I put new bows on my shoes for the dancing class, and wore my new cloak called pearl color, which I bought in Boston at Fox's Store on Cornhill.'

'At four o'clock attended Academy Hall (at Colonel Denny's Hall) with A. Perry. Cousin William Bass of Boston in company with us. Upwards of one hundred and twenty ladies and gents made their appearance and danced until past twelve and then retired; probably

> 'Some pleased and some disgusted,
> Some with rigging maladjusted,
> Some merry, some sad,
> Some sorry, some glad,
> Some elated, others tired,
> Some neglected, others admired,
> Some jovial, some pouting,
> Some silent, some shouting;
> Some are calm, some are crazy,
> Some sprightly, some lazy,
> Some resolved to keep awake,
> Some resolved their sleep to take.
> I am of the lazy crew,
> Sense and nonsense,
> Both adieu!'

At an Academy exhibition in June of 1772 Ruth took the part of Young Lady Lambert in a comedy called 'The Hypocrites.'

Of a trip to Boston, she writes: 'Set out with Daddy in a chaise. Stayed at Mr. Allen's and Salisbury's (Worcester) one hour. Dined at Williams' Tavern at Marlborough at two, lodged at Watertown. In Cambridge called upon Cousin Thomas Denney at Harvard College at six in the morning.

Went with Hannah Bass a-shopping, likewise over Charlestown Bridge to call upon Mrs. Howe, once Rebecca Bass.'

In October, 1793, on another visit to Boston she 'went to the Mall with Dr. and Mrs. Hayward to see the parade which was occasioned by the death of Governor Hancock.

'The procession consisted of several companies of horse, and of artillery, the field pieces covered with black velvet. Drums muffled played the "Dead March" and the band a solemn dirge, preceded by the coffin. The Lieutenant Governor, Secretary, Judges of the Supreme Court, Members of Congress, followed by twenty-one carriages belonging to Boston, made a very elegant and respectable appearance, and the bells tolled.'

'Went with Mr. Bass and daughters to Beacon Hill, where we had a delightful prospect of Boston and neighboring towns. From there went on the new bridge leading from Boston to Cambridge. Took tea at Mr. Bass's, then went up to see Aunt Bass, who is eighty-seven years and in good health. Visited new theatre, from there to Fort Hill, for a view of the harbor.'

'Once more at home,' she records.

'Kept house with fourteen in the family, almost distracted with singing, crying, laughing, talking — and what not.'

'December 31, 1810, reflection.'

'In after years this was reviewed. I now seem to wonder how we survived the drudgery of receiving company or going abroad every day in the year! But we did it for many years.'

On November 4, 1810, Ruth started from Worcester with friends for a trip to Norfolk, Virginia, making the journey by stage-coach as far as Baltimore. After leaving Norfolk, Virginia, she writes:

'Disappointed another lady who ran out with bandbox and

wished to join our party! But we shook our heads and left her standing in the street, and perhaps she is there yet.

'Had a beautiful ride to New York through a part of Harlem, over Harlem Bridge which is very handsome.'

Later she visited Vaux Gardens and 'viewed the machine for raising water for the acqueducts.'

The next afternoon they left for New York and took a sail across the Hudson, continuing their journey by stage on the other side. At Baltimore they took a packet for the sail to Norfolk, where they arrived on November 19, the fifteenth day after leaving Worcester.

On December 24 of that same year, Ruth writes from Norfolk, Virginia: 'We made apple pies for Christmas and other nick-nacks. Guns fired incessantly from four o'clock to midnight to usher in Christmas.'

On the 25th, 'the streets all day mostly filled with negroes, all ages, sizes and figures, dressed in their best, playing and dancing, shaking hands, etc. This and the following five days being the negroes' holidays.

'After this came a kind of market day for slavery, on which they are hired and let, bought and sold like the herds in the stalls.'

After eight months in Virginia she started back on June 23, 1802, sailing for New York in the brig *Alexander* and arriving after a stormy passage on the 30th. By sloop and packet from New York to Providence, thence by stage, she made her homeward journey, arriving at Mr. Moses Bass's in Boston on Monday, July 5. Her cousins had just returned from hearing an oration by Mr. Emerson. All the company went in the evening to view fireworks from the Mall, and the next morning she took the stage at five o'clock from King's Tavern for home.

In 1804, on February 14, Ruth was married to Asa Miles of Westminster, a Dartmouth professor. Doctor Miles lived only a short time thereafter, and in 1806 she married the Reverend Ezekiel L. Bascom. They lived in Deerfield, Fitzwilliam, and Ashby, the last place his longest pastorate, and there both he and his wife are buried.

In the Museum at Ashby are many relics as well as numerous pastel portraits done by Mrs. Bascom. It seems that during this later period of her life she took up the making of silhouettes and pastel portraits, for one of the earliest notices in her journal is of the making of a profile of Susan Rice on September 14, 1819.

'July 11, 1826. Woodward brought the glass and Southgate sent two frames. Put Harriet in the frame.' This may have been Harriet Denny, for she wrote to a relative, 'I have the little red-haired niece with me, and I am doing her picture.' And Harriet Denny's daughter wrote in after years, 'We have one pastel of mother when she was a little girl and value it above rubies.'

Another quotation, dated Boston, 1830:

'Went to some shops on the way to Hanover Street [Doctor Low's], bought some crayons at Burdit's and crayon paper; began to paint the two sisters, Rebecca and Lydia Lovejoy of Nelson, N.H. Painted till twelve and slept little after that for the continually rattling of coaches going and coming on pavements under my windows.'

'July 6, 1837. Painted on little Mary Denny.'

'July 17, 1837. After dinner went to Dr. Holmes' and William Scott's, and finished the painting and framing of twin sisters Woodcock.'

'July 24, 1837, came to Dr. Flint's and began little Stephen Salisbury's sketch.'

'Sept. 8th, I painted Herbert Richardson, ten years old, a neighbor who was sketched last P.M., and then took Miss Knight's shadow at evening.'

These engagements go on for some time in this way. The two sisters who were so kind as to give all this information to me gave a further insight into Ruth Henshaw's character and life, as follows: 'Ruth Henshaw was a clever needlewoman, as well as being expert with her pen and brush. She made and remade both dresses and hats, and was dexterous at spinning and weaving. One of our older cousins wrote some years ago, "Our mother instilled into our childish minds a reverence for her very name."' The sister who wrote all this went on to say, 'There seems to be no description of her personal appearance, except this, from a letter as she appeared in later life: "I have heard it said that she was short, stooped, and with dark eyes."'

Among Ruth's friends at Leicester Academy was a young man, Ethan Allen Greenwood by name, who took part in some of the same programs with her at exhibitions, and was later a guest at her marriage to Doctor Miles. Their mutual interest in portrait painting was another bond between them. (Ethan Allen Greenwood was a very popular artist in those days.)

I regret that as long as there is no picture by Mrs. Bascom in the collection at the picture gallery at Harvard, Massachusetts, I cannot include any copies of portraits of hers I have seen. There are some very fine ones at Leicester, Massachusetts, and they are to be found in various places. There are two at the Concord Antiquarian Society which are typical of her work, but not up to the standard of some others I have seen. She always posed her sitters in profile, but she gets a good likeness, and you feel a certain power behind the stroke of her brush. These portraits must be classed among the primitives, for they are very crude in comparison with some of the other pastels that were painted at that time, but Mrs. Bascom was so well known, and her pictures are so much prized among antiquarians these days, that it is well to look up her work. One of the portraits in the Concord Antiquarian Society has to my mind been made more crude by her having cut gold spectacles out of gilded paper and stuck them onto the portrait! This may be very quaint and odd, but it takes away some of the seriousness from that piece of work, and yet there is something about Mrs. Bascom's portraits that is very appealing.

There were a number of artists among the itinerants who like Ruth Bascom always kept to the profile. Having perfected it they never attempted a full face or even a three-quarter face, and probably would have made a dismal failure of it if they had. Many of them were popular in their day and did good work as far as it went, and in these times their works are prized by collectors. This proves, as has been said before, that it is not the minor details that count as long as the spirit and life latent in the portrait manages to emanate from it.

It is interesting to follow the various types of portraits of that time. Nothing could be further removed from Mrs. Bascom's paintings than the painting of a lady from the old Walter Perkins house in Brookline, Massachusetts. (Page 135.) The family who lived in the house does not know by whom the portrait was painted, but it represents one of their forbears, and is very quaint. The lady is standing close to a rich red curtain that covers half the background. She has on a finely painted velvet dress with a gilt buckle at the waist. She has blue eyes and black hair and a very saucy tip-tilted nose. Around her throat is tied a Neptune-blue ribbon from which stands up a delicate lace frill that goes around her marvellous cap made of enumerable loops of blue ribbon of the same hue as the bow at her throat.

For some reason only known to herself she looks frightened as if she were seeing a ghost. The pupils of her eyes are dilated, and it seems to me that she must have been of a very nervous temperament. But she was very picturesque for all that.

Another portrait (page 136) more or less of this type of the ghost-seeing kind was that of the Reverend Mr. Josiah Waitt. This portrait hung on the walls of the old Sterling

Inn, as the reverend gentleman married the innkeeper's daughter. He must have been a very strange man, for when she died he insisted upon lying down in her coffin to see whether it was comfortable for her! Types of this kind were perfectly possible in old New England towns in those days, the type now having entirely disappeared, and probably the young people of today would find it almost impossible to believe that they ever existed. That is why they are very worth while recording.

Another tale which has the flavor of old New England is this. I came across a portrait (page 137) which had hung for many years in an old house in Pepperell. The painting always awoke in me a certain amount of curiosity, and when I asked where it came from, the lady from whom I got it told me it came from out of a dilapidated house up in the woods, which belonged to a very old man by the name of Kilbourn. The portrait was of a woman of about forty years of age. She wears a black velvet dress, with a white low collar edged with lace falling over a white embroidered chemisette, and white cuffs. Around her neck is wound what looks like a black cord, but which really was a woven cord made of the hair of some 'dearly departed.' These were worn quite frequently in those days. In her hand she holds a green book edged with gilt lines. On her finger is a gold ring, and there is a gold breastpin at her throat. A silver pencil is thrust into her belt like a dagger. In her left hand she holds a pink rose. Her hair is very dark and her eyes are also dark and very striking.

I went in search of that old house, and came upon it suddenly. It looked very, very ancient. A deep sloping roof, with window-sashes filled with the smallest panes of glass I had ever come across. There was something rather gruesome about the house. Perhaps it was the solitude of the place that affected me. Everything about it seemed to have gone to pieces. The chimney leaned to one side. It had sagged as though its age were more than it could carry. A dog, a dread-ful-looking animal, misshapened by age and rheumatism but with a snarling, ferocious face, came creeping down towards me as I stood attempting to take a photograph of the place and its surroundings. The sight of this animal frightened me. I jumped into the motor-car from which I had descended and drove down to the village of Pepperell. A young man was standing on the sidewalk. I stopped and asked him who lived in the old house.

'Oh!' he said, 'that's the house that old Mr. Kilbourn lives in.' Then I knew that was where my picture had come from, and upon inquiry from various townspeople whom I questioned I found out the following tale:

Long ago a very lovely girl named Lucy Orcutt lived on a farm near-by. At that time the farms on the hill were cultivated and cared for; crops grew in the fields and cows grazed in the pastures, and the farms had the air of belonging to well-to-do people.

Now, there was to be a dance in Pepperell one night to which this girl went. It so happened that two young Harvard College students by the names of Leeds and Frothingham, being off on a lark during vacation time, found their way into the village. Hearing that there was a dance going on, they managed to get into the hall, and looking around them they saw numbers of young people dancing and singing and having a good time.

Suddenly they saw a girl coming towards them who was as pretty as a picture. It was Lucy Orcutt. Young Leeds was daring and assured in his manner, and immediately went up to her and asked for a dance. It was no usual thing to see two good-looking young men, evidently gentlemen, at one of these village dances; the girl felt flattered and accepted him as her partner, and away they danced into the middle of the hall. Very soon young Frothingham followed them and claimed Lucy for a dance himself, and as the evening went on they took turns, and none of the other young men had any chance to pay her attention. The more they saw of her, the prettier she looked to them, for her cheeks grew rosier and her eyes danced more brightly from the excitement of this new experience.

The students told Lucy they were leaving the next day, but when the morning came they decided to stay on, and then the romance began. Young Leeds fell desperately in love and sought her company continually. He was the son of a wealthy family in Boston, as was also his friend Frothingham. It was no wonder, therefore, that this simple country girl felt proud and flattered by their attentions, especially that of young Leeds, for he did not hesitate to tell Lucy that he loved her.

To one looking on, it would have seemed as if this was merely the exuberance of youth on Leeds's part, which would quickly cool down, but it did not prove to be so, for he truly wanted Lucy as his wife, and he announced this out of a clear sky by letter to his bewildered family. Then he went and sought them in person. His mother and father told him that such a thing was impossible, that he was too young to begin with to know his own mind, and that such an ill-assorted marriage could not fail to bring unhappiness, not only to him but to the girl as well. He would not listen to them, and without discussing the matter further, he went back to Pepperell and married the girl and brought her to Boston to the luxury of a home at 61 Beacon Street, overlooking the Boston Common. It was the very heart of the fashionable quarter, and Leeds set to work to fit his wife for the position as mistress of so fine a mansion. He gave her everything he could think of to make her happy — beautiful dresses, jewels, etc. The rooms were filled with treasures of art. Any girl would have thought that she had landed in fairyland with so much refinement and beauty around her.

It was not more than a year later when Lucy gave birth to a son, and it must have been a year or so after that that some itinerant artist painted her portrait with her little boy standing on her knee. (Page 138.)

A few years went by, and her young husband was stricken with a fatal illness and died. In view of what followed it would seem that Lucy could never have taken any real place amongst his friends. Of that we do not know. But now she was left with only her little son to comfort her, and together in that great big house she must have felt an overwhelming loneliness; she evidently did, for she began to think of her old home in Pepperell with longing.

One day shortly afterwards the Beacon Street house was put on the market for sale, and Lucy began to collect her things together. She had thought the matter over and decided to go back to the farm. She wandered about the big house choosing the objects she wanted to take with her. It was a varied assortment. There was a very beautiful crystal chandelier in the drawing-room which seemed to her to have come out of fairyland, and there were some crystal sconces on the wall that matched it. She could not resist putting them on her list. Then she selected some beautiful sets of china which she knew her husband had valued, but altogether the list she made was not a long one.

Mr. Frothingham helped her in every way, as he was left in charge of the property which Mr. Leeds had left her.

It must have been a strange feeling to Lucy Orcutt Leeds when she came back to the old home after those few years of such a complete change of scene and environment. It seems that her parents had died, and a man named Kilbourn had taken charge of the farm. This man was essentially a worker of the soil. He had no education. He had nothing to commend him, for he was rough and uncouth, but it is said that he was very handsome, and it was not long before Lucy became his wife. It was not a happy choice, and she was quick to find it out. Her little son became a bone of contention between them, and this man made the child feel it, so much so that after enduring it for a few years the latter ran away and sought out a relative who took pity on him, and she educated him as one of her own. The child harbored resentment against his mother for having married this man. Even in after life he could never understand what made her do it, and I was told that he never made any attempt to see her again. Under the circumstances, this frightened mother was glad. Her new husband's dislike of the boy never lessened. It was happier for him to keep away.

Life now began to take on a very different aspect. Two daughters were born to Lucy as time went on. When she married she and her husband had moved out of her old home and gone to the farm on the hill, but Kilbourn neglected it and took no interest in it and times became hard for them. He never had had any money before. He had only his pay as a farm hand to live on, and now, little by little, all the money Lucy had inherited from Mr. Leeds began to sift through his fingers, and the time came when she was obliged to sell the beautiful things which she had brought from the house on Beacon Street, which had certainly looked strangely odd and out of place in the farmhouse. The crystal chandelier was carted away one day and the sconces followed soon after. She was still a very good-looking woman, though the beauty of youth had passed; one day an itinerant artist came through Pepperell, and it must have been then that she dressed herself up in some of her old finery associated with her affluent days and let him paint her portrait. This was the portrait that I first acquired for the picture gallery at Harvard.

In the meantime, Lucy's older daughter showed every evidence of inheriting her beauty, and Mr. Frothingham, who from time to time came up to see them, became more than interested in her, and suggested taking her away to Boston to educate her. Lucy Kilbourn had learned many things in her sojourn in Boston, and she told him that she would never consent to such a thing unless, in spite of her daughter's extreme youth, he married her before he took her away. He agreed to do this, and so one more lovely girl from Pepperell went to the city as a bride to follow out her destiny.

But it was not to be for long. Though Mr. Frothingham gave her a good home, with all the luxuries and comforts of city life, she could not adjust herself to it. She began to pine and her health began to fail, and one day she packed up her things and went back to the farm. Her husband came frequently to see her, and was kind to her, but it was only too evident that she was sinking into a decline, and before very long she died. After that Mr. Frothingham seems to have disappeared from the picture.

In the meantime, Lucy Kilbourn faced her life with fortitude. It must have been one of great disillusionment, but the old New England spirit upheld her. By that time, the woods were creeping over the meadows and pastures. The land was no longer plowed, fences were broken down, and the desolation of later years began to show itself very painfully.

All the other articles that belonged to her life in Boston had almost gone. Hardly any of the beautiful china had remained, whatever pictures she had had been sold off, and finally she was reduced to taking in washing for the people in the village in order to make both ends meet. She was taxing her strength more than nature could stand. There seemed to be nothing to look forward to in the future. The years in Boston with all the surroundings of luxury must have seemed like a dream to her. Those following were filled with arduous labor. The enthusiasm for life had gone, and her health gave away and she died, leaving her second daughter to face the situation alone with her father.

From that time on it seemed as though nature wanted to cover over all traces of what had been. The old house sagged more and more. The forest crept up farther, until great trees overshadowed it. It dwelt in the perpetual twilight of the woods. The father lived to a great age after having become incapacitated. The daughter who remained with him saw the years pass, isolated from the world, out of reach of any sounds but those of the woods. The desolation was complete.

All this I learned from the old people in Pepperell, Massachusetts, who remembered the tale.

Eventually, the picture of Lucy Orcutt Leeds with her little son standing on her knee came into my possession and now hangs in the picture gallery in Harvard, Massachusetts, near the other one taken of her in later life.

In regard to the portrait of Lucy Orcutt Leeds, I received a letter from the late John Brooks Wheelwright on January 26, 1940, which I will quote:

'Dear Miss Sears,

'Something more than similarity of dress leads me to suppose that the portrait of Lucy Orcutt (Leeds) Kilbourn is by Benjamin Greenleaf of Phippsburg, Maine.... They are all in the Cantonese style.'

Possibly Benjamin Greenleaf was one of the itinerant artists who went through Pepperell at that time, spoken of in a letter from a lady born there. She tells me she has some family portraits that she has inherited that were painted by an itinerant artist in Pepperell. Unfortunately, his name has been lost, but he painted there about one hundred years ago. The men were exceedingly well painted, but she says:

'No one seems to want to see the ladies. While there is much that may be improved in the portraits of the men, the faces of their wives are not so well modelled, and their complexions are unnaturally ruddy. Though grandmother was only about thirty-six, the fashion of the day to wear caps makes her look at least fifty, and her gown suggests the stiffness of sheet iron, deeply corrugated. She told us that Mrs. Judge Prescott (mother of the historian) insisted on lending her a lace collar for the occasion. The artist certainly did much better with frilly caps and lacy collars than necks,

PORTRAIT OF ELIAS TRAFTON OF SWANSEA, MASSACHUSETTS
Painted by William M. S. Doyle in 1820.
(Description, page 117)

PORTRAIT OF SOPHRONIA PERRY TRAFTON OF SWANSEA,
MASSACHUSETTS (SISTER OF THE FAMOUS COMMODORE PERRY)
Painted by William M. S. Doyle in 1820.
(Description, page 117)

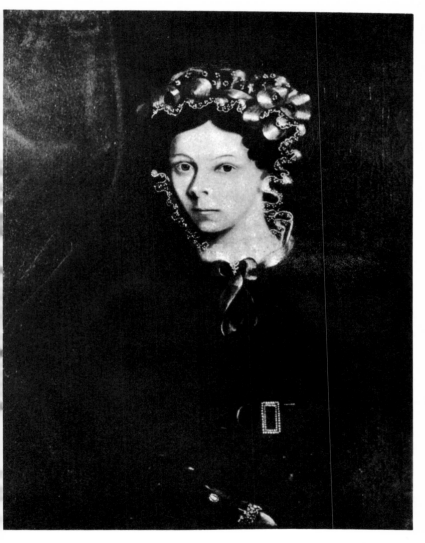

PORTRAIT OF A LADY, FROM THE OLD WALTER PERKINS HOUSE,
BROOKLINE, MASSACHUSETTS
Artist unknown.
(Description, page 125)

[135]

PORTRAIT OF THE REVEREND JOSIAH WAITT OF STERLING,
MASSACHUSETTS
Artist unknown.
(Description, pages 125, 126)

PORTRAIT OF MRS. LUCY ORCUTT LEEDS KILBOURN OF
PEPPERELL, MASSACHUSETTS
Artist unknown.
(Description, page 126)

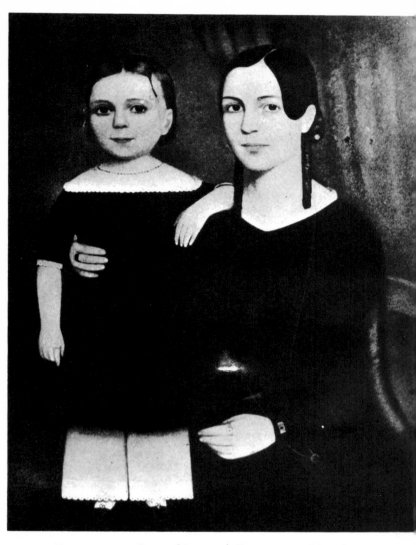

PORTRAIT OF LUCY (ORCUTT) LEEDS AND HER SON
Artist unknown.
(Description, page 129)

[138]

PORTRAIT OF A GENTLEMAN FROM MASSACHUSETTS
Painted by Leonard Burr about 1840.
(Description, page 149)

[139]

PORTRAIT OF HANNAH JACKSON OF BOSTON, MASSACHUSETTS
Artist unknown. Painted in 1843.
(Description, pages 149, 150)

PORTRAIT OF A LADY FROM SALEM, MASSACHUSETTS
Artist unknown.
(Description, page 150)

PORTRAIT OF MISS SARAH A. GOING OF LEOMINSTER,
MASSACHUSETTS
Artist unknown.
(Description, pages 151, 152)

PORTRAIT OF WIDOW MILTON JOSLIN OF WESTMINSTER,
MASSACHUSETTS
Probably painted by Deacon Robert Peckham, about 1840.
(Description, pages 152, 153)

[143]

PORTRAIT OF MRS. DIX OF WESTMINSTER, MASSACHUSETTS
Painted by Deacon Robert Peckham. 1840.
(Description, page 153)

PORTRAIT OF AN OLD LADY FROM ESSEX COUNTY,
MASSACHUSETTS
Artist unknown.
(Description, page 154)

[145]

PORTRAIT OF A LADY FROM ANDOVER, MASSACHUSETTS
Artist unknown.
(Description, page 154)

PORTRAIT OF AN OLD LADY FROM LANCASTER, MASSACHUSETTS
Artist unknown.
(Description, page 154)

PORTRAIT OF MRS. MOORE
Painted by her husband, Mr. A. E. Moore, in 1833.
(Description, page 155)

shoulders, and hands. Great-grandmother's eyes behind her spectacles have a canny look that would be most disconcerting to have constantly following one about the room. We had the ladies out for inspection a few days ago, and returned them, as usual, to their attic retreat.'

Of the artist who painted these portraits, she writes, 'He remained in Pepperell until he had literally "painted up the town." Grandmother said her portrait was painted during the absence of her husband, and that when he returned and saw it his comment was that if she looked like that when he was away he would never dare to leave home again.'

If this artist painted up the town of Pepperell he may be the one that painted the picture of Lucy Orcutt Leeds Kilbourn. Who knows?

And now we leave the portrait of Lucy Orcutt Leeds Kilbourn and go to a rather unique and noticeable portrait (page 139) painted by Leonard Burr of Massachusetts about 1840. It is of a gentleman with greyish hair brushed towards the front, with a fair skin and a rather enigmatic but quizzical face, sitting in a wooden chair made of curly maple, the grain of which stands out noticeably. He wears a black coat with a black satin vest buttoned up the front, with another white-plaited vest under it. His white collar stands high about his chin, and he has a stock of black satin wound around it. In his hands he holds a letter, the wording on the envelope being quite plain, but annoyingly unrevealing.

There is a very charming portrait (page 140) of Miss Hannah Jackson of Boston, Massachusetts, that has a little gayer look than the other, perhaps because she is younger, even though she wears a cap. The background is dark brown with a red curtain draped at one side. She sits in a mahogany chair covered with yellow material. The proverbial black dress is in evidence. Hanging from her neck on a black chain is a gold watch key. The watch is stuck into her belt. She wears a beautiful white muslin collar from Fayal. Her cap surrounds her face and is of muslin with blue bows on it, the ends of which are tied under her chin. In her hand she carries a black book. Her face is very pretty, and she evidently was a woman of refinement. Her coloring is florid, and her hair is coal black in striking contrast to it.

The artist of this portrait is unknown.

Next comes the portrait of a lady from Salem, Massachusetts. (Page 141.) She has a look of the good Queen Elizabeth about her, only better-looking. The picture has a brownish background, and she wears a brown grosgrain silk dress. Around her throat is a very delicate lace ruffle. Her cap is of the same lace and becomingly ruffled around her face with long streamers falling down the front of her dress. Long jewelled earrings drop from her ears. Her hair is dark, and her complexion is florid. She is seated in a red chair.

The artist is unknown.

CHAPTER VI

CAPS, KERCHIEFS, ETC., AND SEA CAPTAINS

Every housewife in the old days had the ambition to own one of the beautiful embroidered collars, kerchiefs, and caps that came from Fayal or Leghorn. They were very exquisite in every way, and it was not everybody who could afford them, but in those times there was sure to be some man in the family sailing the high seas, and when the ships came into Salem Harbor or to any of those harbors along the coast, there was a great deal of commotion and agitation among the womenfolk to see if the cargo contained dainty things from Fayal. The old trunks in the Salem attics were full of them. Lovely bits of delicately embroidered muslin, beautifully done and all by hand, were treasures that were brought out for great occasions. One or more of these things were found in every bride's trousseau if she was fortunate enough to have an uncle or a brother or a father on the incoming ships. These lovely bits of feminine adornment not infrequently drifted into the back country and were donned for the occasion of having a portrait painted.

One of these belonged to a Miss Sarah A. Going of Leominster, Massachusetts. (Page 142.) The collar or kerchief is a marvellous piece of embroidery and painted in a most masterly manner. The cap is also made of the exquisitely embroidered material, and around the crown of it are innumerable loops of iridescent green gauze ribbon. It sets upon the head of a very pretty woman with brown hair and dark eyes. She has on a black, heavy silk dress with a buckle at the waist, and around her neck is a gold chain that seems to be tied in front and falls over the collar. She is evidently sitting upon a sofa and resting her arm upon it, and her hand holds a red book. This hand is very carefully painted, and one feels that the artist had no difficulty in doing it. The background behind the book is made of striped material with a bit of green in it, the exact color of the gauze ribbon in the cap. I heard an artist say, who was examining it at the picture gallery, 'The man who painted that picture was well grounded in the laws of portrait construction,' and he pointed out the fact that the bit of green on the sofa matching the ribbon on the cap balanced and held the whole picture together.

If it could be found who painted this picture, it would unravel a mystery attached to quite a collection of them in that part of the state, for I have come across a number of these caps and kerchiefs that are very beautifully painted. As yet, he has not been unearthed, but sooner or later someone may come along who has a signed picture that corresponds with these, and then the matter will be clarified.

Miss Sarah A. Going married a Mr. Whiting of Shirley, Massachusetts, where she passed her married life. The portrait was acquired through her granddaughter.

Another portrait (page 143) with one of the beautiful caps and kerchiefs is of Mrs. Milton Joslin of Westminster, Massachusetts. Her maiden name was Susan Upton Coe, and she married a man by the name of Doty, and had one or two children by him. She was always looked upon in those days as very much of an aristocrat, and prided herself on her ancestors and the position she held in the community. When Mr. Doty died he left her very well off, and it had not occurred to anybody that she would make a second try at matrimony, but unfortunately she did, and this time she married a Mr. Joslin. He proceeded to spend all the money that he could lay hands on. When he died her affairs were found in a deplorable condition, and she had to curtail her mode of living more and more until finally she became almost destitute. She was then known as 'the Widder Joslin.' Friends and relatives seemed to melt away from her, and she had to rely on the bounty of some of her kindly neighbors. What became of her wonderful collar and cap no one knows. The dress she wears in the portrait is of heavy black silk. Around the cap is twisted white grosgrain ribbon with borders of green, the ties of which fall from under her chin almost down to her waist. The tip of a red chair just shows behind her shoulder. She has a clear-cut face and brown hair, evidently a 'brown front,' which gave her a very hard expression. The portrait was not signed.

Another portrait of her, when she was Mrs. Doty and much younger, hangs in the library at Westminster, Massachusetts. This was painted by Deacon Peckham. As to whether he painted her as Mrs. Joslin is yet to be discovered. The portrait has a very decided Dutch influence about it that is very noticeable. A reason to think it was by Peckham is its general similarity to a portrait of Mrs. Dix (page 144), who was painted by him, and who is dressed in more or less the same manner — the black dress, embroidered collar, the finely done embroidered cap with green iridescent loops of ribbon with ends falling down over her dress. This lady also came from Westminster, and was evidently a person of some consequence. Her erect carriage gives her the appearance of being so.

The similarity of these collars, caps, and kerchiefs is quite bewildering. There is a portrait of a lady from Leominster who again wears the same type of black silk dress, and her embroidered beruffled cap has the same green iridescent loops on it with a very perky bow beside her chin. Her collar is of the same type of embroidered muslin, and this takes us back to the portrait of Miss Sarah A. Going, whose cap also has that same type of ribbon on it. Now, as to whether Peckham painted all these portraits cannot as yet be ascertained with certainty, but it is more than likely, and he may have furnished that same dress and those same ribbons to all. Another point is that the hair in each case is evidently a 'brown front,' and dressed pretty much the same way. The portrait of 'Widder Joslin,' however, is the only one that shows the Dutch influence.

There is another portrait of an old lady from Essex County, Massachusetts, of a different style of painting. (Page 145.) She has on a beruffled mop cap closed at the back and tied in a neat muslin bow under her chin. This cap is not made of the embroidered Fayal muslin, but it is embroidered just the same, and her white muslin kerchief is held neatly down with a V-shaped neck of her black dress. She has brown hair parted in the middle and a severe face, yet a sense of humor lurks in her eyes, which are fine and far-seeing. She is typical of an old New Englander, and I suspect might take a 'nightcap' before going to sleep. The portrait is valuable in so far as it shows a type that has almost died out but was very prevalent in the old days 'up country.'

Still another type of cap can be seen on the portrait of a lady from Andover, Massachusetts. (Page 146.) The ruffle that surrounds her face and the muslin ties are tied under her chin, and muslin loops build the cap up on top of her head. She too wears a 'brown front,' and has a fine motherly face. Over her black dress she had a little old-fashioned shawl. This is a most charming portrait of an old lady, and was chosen by a newspaper critic as one to illustrate the quaint characters whose portraits are shown in the collection, as they appeared in an article of a Boston newspaper.

And still another type of cap is shown in the portrait of a lady of Lancaster, Massachusetts. (Page 147.) She has on an embroidered kerchief over a black dress, and a very full ruffle of white muslin surrounds her face, while the strings of the cap are tied under her chin. This cap has a higher crown at the back, and is certainly very picturesque. I found this portrait behind a sofa covered with innumerable boxes in an old house in West Boylston, Massachusetts, but the portrait came from Lancaster originally.

Another portrait is of Mrs. Moore (page 148), painted on a wooden panel by her husband, A. E. Moore, in 1833. She is a lovely old lady, full of dignity and charm, with brown hair and dark hazel eyes, and a beautiful plaited cap of organdy, very full, with ends tied under her chin. She has a very high ruffle around her neck. One catches a glimpse of a string of small gold beads, but the very unique feature of this portrait is that she wears glasses with steel rims, and against her temples is an extra pair of glasses, presumably for reading. This is the first time I have ever come across anything of that kind.

A very striking portrait (page 165) is one of Mrs. Littlefield of Salem, Massachusetts, the grandmother of the late Doctor Littlefield of Dorchester, Massachusetts. Unfortunately, the artist is unknown. She, too, has on a lovely cap. It is set upon her dark brown hair, which is parted in the middle and waved and curled over the ears. The cap is of the Dutch type, made of lovely sheer embroidery, and the sides stick out slightly behind her waved hair. There is a greenish-yellowish embroidery on the cap which makes it very ornamental. Mrs. Littlefield has rather high coloring, but a very pretty and refined face and beautiful figure, which is well shown off by her long-waisted black dress, and long tight sleeves with two rows of fringe below the shoulders. She has on a small sheer embroidered collar, caught with a small old-fashioned gold brooch, and from around her neck hangs a long fine gold chain with a key on the end of it. The chain is caught with a clasp over the breast. She holds a white fan in her hand. Over her right arm and falling on the chair is a rust-red shawl with a long fringe. There is a ring on her finger. All this has a dark brown background.

One of the oldest portraits in the collection is that of Cloe Hallowell, of Hallowell, Maine, painted by William P. Codman of Boston in 1805. (Page 166.) Cloe is a rather dishevelled little woman. However, she has fine eyes that look out from the picture at you with keen observance. Her cap and kerchief differ in style from the others. They are made of lace. She wears a red satin dress tempered by shadows. The picture is well painted and very mellow in color. The artist, William P. Codman, did most of his portraits in Massachusetts and Maine. He advertised in the *Boston Agricultural Intelligence* as a painter of portraits.

There is a portrait of Mrs. Dyer of Somerville (page 167) which shows a collar that is worth while mentioning, also a beautiful white muslin cap with lace edging. A muslin bow with numerous loops on top crowns this cap. The very broad, plain collar is caught with a small gold-and-black enamel brooch. Her dress is dull black silk, probably grosgrain, with very full sleeves. Both of her hands are showing, and one of them holds a book. She has coal-black hair parted in the middle and puffed out over the ears. The collar is just the shape of that of Mrs. Joyce, mentioned in the early part of this chapter, and the cap is edged with the same lace. Even the dress is the same, although the buckle at the waist is missing. Mrs. Dyer looks as if she might be the daughter of Mrs. Joyce, and as if the artist put them into the same clothes. One naturally would say that this could hardly be, because Mrs. Dyer came from Somerville and Mrs. Joyce was away up in Westminster, but perhaps Mrs. Dyer married a Somerville man. Who can tell?

The portrait of a lady of Salem, Massachusetts (page 168), is one that is apt to attract attention, which is rather strange because there is nothing conspicuous about it. But one look at the face sets one thinking. If Dickens had chosen her to illustrate his character, Rosa Dartle, he could not have found a better model. Underneath a demure exterior one suspects a suspicious, jealous nature. The face is thin and pale and rather good-looking. As she stands partly shielded by the red curtain it looks as though she were eavesdropping and hearing things not meant to be heard. One could also see in her a character of Hawthorne's. She might easily have lived in the House of Seven Gables. The artist of this portrait is unknown, I regret to say.

Another portrait is that of 'A Lady with a Ruff.' Instead of a cap she wears a high tortoise-shell comb at the back of her head. A large ruff surrounds her throat. Her dress is black satin. It is a very pleasing portrait and well painted, but like the other one, the artist's name is a mystery.

The portrait (page 170) listed as being found in an outlying farm near Groton, Massachusetts, is one that is universally liked among the visitors. This is the portrait of a widow, and her cap is an interesting one, as it was the kind that all widows wore in England at that time. I had a great-aunt, Mrs. Francis Peabody, who lived for many years in England, and she always wore a cap of just that shape for the rest of her life after her husband died, only it was made of very crisp and delicate white crêpe and framed the face with pleated folds, exactly like the cap in this portrait. This widow is dressed in a black dress made after the prevailing fashion, full skirt and full sleeves, etc. Her cap is made of a material that looks heavier than muslin. It is tied under her chin. She has a delightfully sympathetic face. The artist is unknown.

One of the most beautiful collars of all is in the portrait (page 171) of Mary Winship, wife of Sea Captain Winship of Melrose, Massachusetts, painted about 1842. I wish so much that I knew of the artist who painted this, for it is very carefully done, and except that it is rather stiff in pose, it is a fine bit of painting. Mary Winship has brown hair piled upon the top of her head in puffs and curls, and two tortoise-shell combs stand up from the top. The effect is truly remarkable. She wears a brown dress and a beautiful Fayal collar. This is as

fine a piece of work as regards detail as could be found anywhere. Pinning the two ends of the collar together at the
throat is an amethyst brooch. Around one wrist is a velvet
ribbon fastened by a gold buckle. There are two rings on her
fingers, and she is holding a red book. The chair she is sitting
in is black with red sides to it.

It is evident from this picture that the sea captains' wives
were quite opulent in appearance. A seafaring life was a re-
munerative one in those days, and when returning from a long
voyage, the captains took pride in dressing up their 'better
halves' with all the finery they had acquired when in foreign
ports.

A letter I received from a lady in Fitchburg, Massachusetts,
is worth quoting. She was talking to an auctioneer there and
asked him if old estates ever turned in family portraits. 'Oh,
yes!' he replied. 'Dozens of them.' She asked him what he
did with them. 'Burn them — burn them!' he replied. 'What!
Burn them?' she said. 'Yes,' he answered. 'I can't have all
those faces staring at me!' How fortunate it is that there are
some who did not follow suit!

Another lady, writing from Lincoln, Massachusetts, says:
'I have in my possession a portrait of my aunt that her
grandfather had painted of her in 1853 by one of these itinerant painters when she was five years old. The face is a very
good likeness, but the whole thing is very set, and too
wooden-looking for a child. She stands holding in one hand
a basket and a rose in the other, which must have been a
favorite posture with the painter, as there is another portrait
in town in the same position. Her pink dress is made very
full and cut with a low neck from the top of the shoulders
with a lace edge at the top to finish it, and gathered with a
belt at the waist. Pantalettes hang below the dress, and she
wears low black laced shoes. Her hair is a Dutch cut. My
mother said that her grandfather paid five dollars to have it
painted, and in those days that must have seemed quite a sum.'

Another very beautiful cap one finds in the portrait of a lady from Leominster (page 172), probably painted by Deacon Robert Peckham about 1840. The cap is comprised of two rows of delicate lace standing out full about the face. On the top is a very smart bow of pale green iridescent gauze ribbon lighting like a butterfly on the top of her head. Around her throat and tied in a jaunty bow by her left cheek is this same pale green ribbon. She has on a beautiful collar of embroidery and lace. Her dress is of black satin, and it is rather a curious fact, but one to be noticed, that all the ladies painted in that part of the state seem to be wearing a dress of this style.

A rather striking portrait (page 173) of the daughter of this lady, as did that of the mother as well, came out of an old house in Leominster, Massachusetts, on the walls of which they had hung for many long years. The daughter has coal-black hair, parted in the middle with bunches of curls on either side of her face and with a big roll of hair on top of her head. She has large black eyes that look out from under heavy eyebrows. Her dress is of red silk with a handsome buckle at the waist, and she is the proud possessor of a collar from Fayal.

Following (page 174) is a portrait of a gentleman taken from the old house in Leominster, with those of his wife and daughter, recorded above. It was probably painted by Robert Peckham in 1843.

A gentleman writing to me from Worcester, Massachusetts, about the portraits of his paternal grandparents, which were executed in Lowell, Massachusetts, in 1838 ('This refers to the portraits and not the subjects!' he writes), gave the following information:

'The main fact disclosed was that this was the first year of their marriage when they had just set up housekeeping, and before the first of the family of nine children had arrived. They paid thirty dollars for the two portraits, an extravagance which they never failed to wonder over after a full half-century. The interesting thing was that they both denied that either picture had carried any likeness of the original. My grandfather said he never owned anything resembling the wardrobe in which he appeared dressed in the portrait! They were unable to recall the name of the painter, but some later investigation of my own led me to believe that he might have been Thomas B. Lawson.'

A lady wrote me from Oxford, Massachusetts:

'We have in our family a painting by a man that went through town painting portraits. He stopped at my great-grandfather's tavern. This portrait painter could not pay for his board, so painted a picture of my grandmother. I am quite sure the artist is Hanson. My grandmother never would have the picture hung on the wall while she was alive. She said it did not look like her at all, but after she had passed away, my father had it hung in our parlor. It was always in the attic until then. My father had just passed away, and my brother in speaking of the picture said he guessed it would go back into the attic. This is all I can say about the picture.'

Though this is diverging from caps and kerchiefs, I should like to quote from a letter I received from a lady in Salem. She writes:

'About sixty-nine or seventy years ago when we were small children, a man came to our house for a meal. My father, who was a man of sterling qualities, recognized him as a man of character.

'My father allowed him to stay over night. He made himself very useful, and without bidding stayed for two years. At the time he disappeared he was as much a mystery as when he came, but one thing may be said about him. He paid well for his keep.

'There were three girls and two boys in our family besides mother and father. Charlie could help my father around the barn and house. My father was a peddler. He mended umbrellas and sold jewelry, and had a store on Essex Street in

Salem, and at another time on Central Street, but Charlie Purdy could be trusted with valuables, family, and children, although what may be termed a shiftless person, not making use of his talents.

'In our house he could cook, sew, mend, patch, make pants, cut men's suits, stylish cut, and could paint or draw a portrait of any person and enjoy doing this, but never tried to make money. He could paint beautiful scenery also. For a man so talented, and of such sterling qualities, we always remembered him as a man who may have been famous. But he left us as unceremoniously as he came, we know not whither he went. But if this is the man you are looking for, he impressed our childish minds as being a real "he-man," and we know he had talent uncommercialized.

'This was Charlie Purdy. He could paint your portrait as real as life, or make a beautiful sunset. We have none of his pictures. As I remember him as a child of eight, the oldest he could be when he left was about thirty. Maybe he was older or younger, as children are poor judges of age.'

This description of Charlie Purdy, who painted a number of portraits in Salem, was exceedingly interesting to me to receive, as I well remember my Grandfather Peabody's telling me about this mysterious man who never let on who he was, but who could paint exceedingly well. He went to see my grandfather a number of times, and he evidently was a very quaint character in his day.

When one comes upon something by surprise, there is a double charm to it. That is what I felt when I came upon the portrait of the lady with a great cap on. (Page 175.) Such a structure of loops of gauze ribbon would be difficult to duplicate. She is young and pretty, with dark, appealing eyes and a very winsome smile, and she holds her head high under her great cap. She wears a black velvet dress, cut low in the neck, and a string of red coral beads with an amber pendant attached and coral earrings which give light and color to the picture. Her brown hair is parted in the middle and curled and puffed out on either side of her face. The artist is unknown.

In Marblehead, Newburyport, and other coast towns there was a great demand among the families of sea captains for portraits by itinerant portrait painters. The captains were usually painted before going on one of their long voyages to the East.

J. G. Cole, William Prior, and Zedekiah Belknap painted many of these portraits, and in an article named 'Hawkers and Walkers in Early America,' by Richardson Wright, the statement is made that Isaac Sheffield of New London, Connecticut, 'specialized on portraits of sea captains. They were all painted with red faces, all stand before a red curtain, and each holds in his hand a single telescope. Sheffield was gathered to his fathers in 1845, but his works survive him.'

Here is an anecdote from that locality that is worth telling. A tale goes that one of these itinerant artists planned a trip to some of the seacoast towns, and being forehanded painted on a number of canvases the figures of sea captains, and some clergymen, because parishes were always eager to have a portrait of their pastor. Thus armed he set forth. He was so successful with the sea captains whom he approached first that he ran out of canvases on which they were portrayed, so he took one that was already painted for a clergyman and painted a sea captain over it.

All went well for some time. The clergyman disappeared and the captain reigned triumphantly, but it was not for so very long. There came a day when the clergyman began to reappear on the canvas. The artist had not put the paint used for the sea captain on thick enough. The family was greatly distressed. Day after day they looked at it and clearer and clearer they saw the clergyman. A feeling of resentment took hold. They began to think that the neighbors might become distrustful of the sea captain. It looked as though he were a sort of Doctor Jekyll and Mr. Hyde. The sea captain himself became quite agitated over it, and began to be superstitious. Things got so bad that one day after viewing the picture, the family hurriedly took it up to the garret and hid it away behind an old trunk, and when no one was around they went stealthily up and destroyed it.

And this reminds me of a letter I received on April 30, 1939, from a lady in Newtonville, Massachusetts, who took one of her old family portraits to the Fogg Art Museum of Harvard University to have it restored. The gentleman who did the restoring took considerable interest in it and, she writes:

'After he had cleaned it and straightened out the canvas, he showed me a few things that he had found, namely some blue on the edge of the coat and white cravat, and two or three yellowish spots showing through the dark color of the coat at points where buttons might have been.

'His interpretation was to this effect: that the itinerant portrait painters carried around with them stock canvases with the figures already on them, so it was necessary only to add the head and hands of the person whose portrait was being painted, and possibly also slight alterations in the figure. He thought the painter of this portrait might have run out of civilian figures and had used a uniformed one, possibly a naval figure, which he painted over.'

It shows that this trick was one to be avoided, as it might easily lead to ghost stories and scare people out of their wits.

The portraits of sea captains in the picture gallery at Fruitlands are well painted and very picturesque. The one painted by Cole (page 176) (probably either Lyman Emerson Cole or Charles Octavius Cole, both of Newburyport, Massachusetts) has a reddish-brown background. The red plush sofa or chair upon which the captain is sitting is edged with a gold ball fringe. He has beautiful blue eyes and dark brown hair brushed to the front and he wears a dark blue navy coat, with large brass buttons and a velvet collar standing rather high at the back. His vest is a brownish brocade and braided in scallops on the edge. Beneath the brocaded vest is another one of white, and he wears a very high white collar with a white stock around it.

The portrait (page 177) of Sea Captain Randolph of Portsmouth, New Hampshire, painted by Zedekiah Belknap, is quite a forceful production. The captain is very dark with flashing black eyes, and looks as if he might have sailed on the high seas through a number of successful and adventurous voyages. He is still young, and undoubtedly had many years before him when this picture was painted. He has dark brown hair, brushed to the front, and wears a typical sea captain's coat, white collar, vest, and cravat.

Zedekiah Belknap painted as early as 1810 in Massachusetts. He was a man of some education, having graduated from Dartmouth College in 1807. He evidently was popular, for one comes across his portraits every now and then, made especially along the seacoast. He died in Weathersfield, Vermont.

The portrait (page 178) of Captain Greeley, who was a sea captain and a shipbuilder, and a man of prominence in his profession, was painted by Joseph Greenleaf Cole in 1826. This portrait came from the old Greeley homestead at Ellsworth, Maine. There were many beautiful things in that old house, but some of them had to be sold during the years of depression, and this picture was bought right off the wall where it had hung for a great many years.

Joseph Greenleaf Cole was the son of Moses D. Cole. He was born in Newburyport in 1803. After studying with his father for a few years (his father being a painter himself), he came to Boston and died in 1858. He painted many portraits, one of the best of which is that of George R. T. Hewes, belonging to the Bostonian Society and hung for years in the Old State House in Boston. (Fielding's *Dictionary of American Painters*.)

Captain Greeley was a very fine-looking man. The seafaring

PORTRAIT OF MRS. LITTLEFIELD OF SALEM, MASSACHUSETTS
Artist unknown. Painted about 1840.
(Description, page 155)

[165]

PORTRAIT OF CLOE HALLOWELL OF HALLOWELL, MAINE
Painted by William P. Codman of Boston, Massachusetts, in 1805.
(Description, page 156)

[166]

PORTRAIT OF MRS. DYER OF SOMERVILLE, MASSACHUSETTS
Artist unknown.
(Description, page 156)

[167]

PORTRAIT OF A LADY OF SALEM, MASSACHUSETTS
Artist unknown.
(Description, pages 156, 157)

PORTRAIT OF THE WIFE OF MAJOR X OF BENNINGTON, VERMONT
Artist unknown.   Painted between 1838 and 1845.
(Description, pages 190, 191)

PORTRAIT FROM AN OUTLYING FARM IN GROTON,
MASSACHUSETTS

Artist unknown. Painted about 1840.
(Description, page 157)

[170]

PORTRAIT OF MARY WINSHIP, WIFE OF SEA CAPTAIN WINSHIP
OF MELROSE, MASSACHUSETTS

Artist unknown. Painted about 1842.

(Description, pages 157, 158)

[171]

PORTRAIT OF A LADY FROM LEOMINSTER, MASSACHUSETTS
Probably painted by Deacon Robert Peckham about 1840.
(Description, page 159)

[172]

PORTRAIT OF A YOUNG WOMAN IN A RED DRESS FROM
LEOMINSTER, MASSACHUSETTS
(DAUGHTER OF THE LADY FROM LEOMINSTER)
Probably painted by Deacon Robert Peckham in 1840.
(Description, page 159)

[173]

PORTRAIT OF A GENTLEMAN, TAKEN FROM THE OLD HOUSE IN
LEOMINSTER WITH THOSE OF HIS WIFE AND DAUGHTER
Probably painted by Deacon Robert Peckham in 1843.
(Description, page 159)

[174]

PORTRAIT OF A LADY WITH A GREAT CAP, FROM BOSTON,
MASSACHUSETTS

Artist unknown.   Painted about 1835.

(Description, pages 161, 162)

[175]

PORTRAIT OF A NEWBURYPORT SEA CAPTAIN
Painted by Cole (either Lyman Emerson Cole or Charles Octavius Cole, both of Newburyport), between 1830 and 1840.
(Description, pages 163, 164)

PORTRAIT OF SEA CAPTAIN RANDOLPH OF PORTSMOUTH,
NEW HAMPSHIRE

Painted by Zedekiah Belknap in 1839.

(Description, page 164)

PORTRAIT OF SEA CAPTAIN GREELEY OF ELLSWORTH, MAINE
Painted by Joseph Greenleaf Cole in 1826.
(Description, pages 164, 181)

PRE-REVOLUTIONARY PORTRAIT OF SEA CAPTAIN HALLETT OF
LONG ISLAND, NEW YORK
Artist unknown.
(Description, page 181)

PORTRAIT OF A GENTLEMAN, DISCOVERED HIDDEN IN THE LOFT
OF A BARN IN STOUGHTON, MASSACHUSETTS

Artist unknown.

(Description, pages 184, 185)

[180]

life had somewhat toughened his complexion, which was florid. His hair was brown with a reddish tint to it, and brushed forward, as seemed to have been the fashion of the day, and he wore what were then called 'sideburns.' His eyes were blue. He was taken holding a wooden measuring instrument. He wears a black coat, with large brass buttons, a vest of brown striped brocade with a white lace jabot, and a high white collar and white cuffs.

One of the most interesting portraits of sea captains is that of Captain Hallett of Long Island, New York, a pre-Revolutionary portrait. (Page 179.) Half of the background is rock and trees and the rest is the sea with a murky sky. Close to the horizon is his three-masted schooner, full sail, flying the Union Jack.

Captain Hallett wears his hair in a queue. He is a fine-looking son of the sea, with a ruddy face, and somewhat weather-beaten. He wears a stone-grey coat with large buttons and a white vest. Out from his sleeve comes a frill of thin white material that half-covers his hand, which holds a single telescope. The portrait has a decidedly Dutch influence permeating it.

The reason for this portrait's being placed with all these of New England is to show that in each section of the country the itinerants had their own peculiar way of painting, each differing distinctly from the others. The portraits painted in New York State were quite different from those in New England or Pennsylvania or the Southern States. They all had their particular style.

CHAPTER VII

A PORTRAIT of a lady (page 197) by P. Hewins that hangs in the picture gallery at Harvard, Massachusetts, has raised a controversy among quite a number of the people who have seen it. It is a very charming portrait, and is always noticed. Very frequently people exclaim when they see it, 'Oh, there is a portrait by Amasa Hewins!' and they take exception to the label which is on it stating that it is by P. Hewins. They claim that I must have made a mistake, but I explain that his signature is signed P. Hewins, and he must have known what his name was, but that seems to make little impression, for they say that it is in the style of Amasa Hewins, and must be one of his pictures. Finally, one gentleman came along who became quite agitated on the subject, because in some way Amasa Hewins was related to his family, and he said that he could not mistake his style anywhere. As usual, I said it was signed by P. Hewins, and he said he did not know that there was any such person as P. Hewins, and that this picture was so unmistakably by Amasa Hewins that I ought to put a note next to it explaining about it. One day when he was there still expostulating, a relative, I'm not sure it was not a son, came into the gallery, and catching sight of this portrait exclaimed, 'Well, there is an Amasa Hewins, and no mistake!' And they both said the error ought to be rectified.

All this began to make me rather unsettled about it. I inquired around in many places as to whether anybody had heard of P. Hewins, and always the same answer came back: 'You are thinking of Amasa Hewins. I don't believe there is a P. Hewins.' Finally I got a letter from a lady in Dedham who wrote: 'In this town there are several portraits by Amasa Hewins in the possession of his grandchildren. He was born in Dedham and died in Florence, Italy,' and she goes on to suggest that I write to one of them for further particulars. I still held my ground and insisted that a man must know his own name. Soon after that I got the following letter from a lady from Bath, Maine:

'My brother saw an exhibition of itinerant painters recently in Boston. [They were exhibited in the Doll and Richards Gallery before they were installed at Harvard.] One picture by P. Hewins he noticed especially, as we have a portrait of Abigail Hopkins painted by P. Hewins in 1836. If at any time you are motoring through Bath, we shall be very glad to show it to you.

'Very sincerely yours,
'(Signed) ——'

That established the portrait as being under the right name.

These experiences are sometimes quite difficult to cope with, but I felt very much pleased at the way this one came out. The portrait in question is of a very showy, dark-eyed lady with a gorgeous green watered-silk dress cut low in the neck with short sleeves. Her coal-black hair is as gleaming as a raven's wing. She has high coloring and very red lips.

'Philip Hewins was born in Blue Hill, Maine, in 1806. In 1834 he established a studio in Hartford, Connecticut, where he lived until his death in 1850. His portraits were pronounced good likenesses.' (Fielding's *Dictionary of American Painters*.)

In contrast to this rather dashing portrait there is a lovely portrait (page 198) of a delicate young girl, Miss Wyman of Winchendon, Massachusetts. This came from the late Gamaliel Beaman of Princeton, Massachusetts, who was a very old gentleman and had been a collector all his life, and was considered an authority in such matters. He told me all about her and her family. The portrait was painted by Dobson, who was very popular in that part of the state, and Mr. Beaman said he was considered a very good portrait painter. This portrait shows that, for the color is very harmonious and it is well painted. The background is a shaded brown. The girl has a lovely natural complexion, brown eyes, brown hair in ringlets framing the face. Her dress is snuff brown with full sleeves falling off from the shoulder and is piped with narrow lace. The cuffs are of white muslin. Over her shoulders is loosely thrown a sheer scarf of rose color which is tied over the breast. She holds an open book in her hand, which shows some wording on it.

It is very difficult sometimes to find out anything about these old artists. One has to go through innumerable volumes of art dictionaries, etc., and then we may find only one for all our trouble. The writers of these dictionaries evidently had their favorites, for one may find the name of an out-of-the-way artist, and then be much surprised to find that of a well-known artist left out. Such investigation requires a great deal of time and research.

There is a mystery about the portrait of a gentleman (page 180) which was discovered in the loft of an old barn at Stoughton, Massachusetts. It had lain there hidden by the hay for a great many years, and the barn had changed owners several times. Whether they had found it out or knew nothing about it cannot be ascertained, but a photographer in searching around the building discovered it. The present owner apparently knew it was there but did not know the history of it, who the subject was, or who owned it. It was very evident that it was a good portrait and that of a gentleman. I got wind of its existence, and made some inquiries about it. The owner at first had evidently feared getting into trouble if he sold it, but after consulting various people, he was assured that the picture's having been there for so many years without being claimed gave him the right to dispose of it.

The background is brown, and the subject is sitting in a carved mahogany chair, dressed in a black frock coat, white vest buttoned down the front, and a high white collar with a stock wound around it and tied in a bow in front. He has a gold ring on his little finger. His hair is black and is cut close to his head, brushed to the front, giving a windblown effect. His eyes are blue. He was evidently a very well set-up gentleman, for he carries a pair of grey kid gloves in his hand. The artist is unknown.

There is a portrait in the gallery at Harvard of Mrs. Helen Bradbury (page 199) which in style is very typical of those days. She was of Buxton, Maine. She was a grandmother of Lawyer Moore of Swampscott, Massachusetts, and is very picturesque with her brown hair, which has been curled over a wooden curling-stick, hanging in long bunches on either side of her face, with a pug piled on top of her head, and brown-shell side combs. Her white lace cuffs show out well on her snuff-colored brown dress. She has a ring on her first finger, and she holds a rose. The artist of this portrait is also unknown. It is well worth a place in the gallery.

Some of the most prized portraits of the artists of that time are those of Albert Gallatin Hoit. One of these hangs in the gallery. It is a portrait of Susan Pierce Jarvis (later Mrs. Joseph Thornton Adams of Claremont, New Hampshire). (Page 221.) This was painted by Hoit in 1830, when she was a bride. She is taken sitting by the window in the old Jarvis Homestead in Claremont. A view of Ascutney Mountain can be seen through the window. The old house is still standing now, having been bought by a lady and restored sufficiently to live in without hurting the original plan. The window at which Susan Jarvis was sitting just before her marriage is still there, with the wooden shutter against which she was leaning just as it was.

[185]

Susan's father was a very important man in that part of New Hampshire, being a well-known physician. He owned many acres of land. The wedding of his daughter took place in the village church. As the portrait shows, the bride was a very lovely young woman with her brown hair piled high upon her head, and it is said that the bridegroom was a very good-looking young man. On the back of the portrait was pasted an account of the wedding, and a poem written by her bridesmaids, as follows:

The Young Bride

The village church, at evening sun,
　　Was throng'd from far and near;
Few heard the bell — but rumors run,
　　The Bride was to appear.

From mountain, glen, and riverbank,
　　The villagers were there;
And beaming eyes were waiting long,
　　To greet the bridal pair.

They enter'd soon the hallow'd dome,
　　Advancing up the aisle;
And to the altar, as they came,
　　Were cheer'd by many a smile.

Her dress was like the driven snow,
　　The emblem of her mind;
For taste and spotless purity
　　Were happily combined.

Her lightsome step and modest gaze
　　Spoke dignity and youth;
And ev'ry feature of her face
　　Display'd a heart of truth.

Her beaming eye, that oft had roam'd
　　With careless glance around,
Now seem'd with deep emotion fill'd,
　　And bent upon the ground.

Her face, that oft with sunny smiles
Had charmed each ranging eye,
Now shed a gentler pale and red,
As mild as summer sky.

'Twas doubtful, then, which most,
The lily or the rose;
For both were there alternately,
As each spectator knows.

They kneel'd before the holy fane,
To pledge unchanging love;
And Heaven knew the vows were
As those enroll'd above.

He plac'd the ring upon her hand —
Emotion deep revealing;
Each witness felt a sympathy,
While wedded fate was sealing.

And now before the altar bent,
The circle join'd in prayer;
And each a benediction lent,
To bless the wedded pair.
                                CLARIGENETTE
Claremont, *August* 31, 1830

One can picture the scene in this old country church with all the neighbors flocking around the bride and groom and congratulating them both when the service was over. They probably drove off in an old-fashioned chaise while the bridesmaids threw slippers after them, and the old people stood behind with tears in their eyes, yet happy in their happiness. All this I seem to see as I read the little old poem faded with age, adding so much to the interest of the portrait.

The announcement of the marriage appeared in the *Vermont Republican and Journal* of September 11, 1830. Then on September 30 the young couple were married by the Reverend Mr. Howe. The notice in the paper read this way:

Mr. Joseph Thornton Adams, M.D., editor of the *Columbian Sentinel*, Boston, to Miss Susan P. Jarvis, daughter of Dr. Leonard Jarvis, Claremont, N.H.

Susan Jarvis, the bride, was born in 1809 and died in 1848. She had four children by this marriage.

The artist of this portrait, Albert Gallatin Hoit, 'was born in Sandwich, New Hampshire, in 1800. He died in 1856. After he gathered enough funds he was able to go to France and to Italy, and he studied there. On his return he settled in Boston, where he painted many portraits. He became first president of the Boston Art Club, and he painted a very successful full-length portrait of Daniel Webster which is owned by the Union League Club of New York.' (Fielding's *Dictionary of American Painters*.)

A portrait (page 200) which is painted in still another style is that of Mrs. O. E. S. Frinck of Medford, Massachusetts. A grey taffeta curtain is pulled aside to show the bluish-grey background. She sits in a carved walnut chair. Her black velvet dress is buttoned down the front, and slipping off one shoulder is a brick-red cape with a yellow lining. Her black hair is parted in the middle, and on either side of her face are long ringlets showing traces of grey. On top of her head the hair is pulled up high into a knot. Her eyes are hazel grey and her teeth are showing. This portrait was painted by her husband, who was a landscape painter as well as a portrait painter.

I have come across several portraits painted by the itinerants that present the subjects showing their teeth. William Thompson Bartoll's picture of Mrs. Bessom (page 224) is painted that way, and there is one by Francis Alexander which will be described later. This was done with the idea of making a person look more natural, and less stiff and severe.

To show the variety in these portraits of different artists, one is mentioned here that is completely different from any of the others. (Page 201.) The young woman was from Owl's

Head, Maine. She was the daughter of the lighthouse-keeper, and in the background can be seen the lighthouse in which she was brought up. It stands on the edge of a cliff with a mountain back of it, and there are green and brown trees in the picture with grass in the foreground. The woman is seated on a rustic chair. Her black hair is parted in the centre with ringlets framing her face. She has high coloring and high cheekbones, showing every evidence of having Indian blood in her veins. She has on a black taffeta dress, with black velvet bands and pipings on the sleeves, bodice, and across the shoulders. The bodice is plaited. The skirt is very full, and the sleeves are flowing and bell-shaped, edged with beautiful coarse lace. The same lace is around the high neck, and at her throat is a large cameo brooch with a gold setting from which hangs a chain that falls into her lap. Around her wrist is a gold bracelet with a short chain, and a gold wedding ring is on her fourth finger, while on her first finger is an old-fashioned ring set with pearls. The paint in this picture has been put on in a very smooth way, making the portrait look almost like a water-color. The lace and the dress are remarkably well painted, as is so often to be found in these portraits of itinerant painters. The artist is unknown. The portrait was presented to the collection by Mr. C. E. Merrill, of Newton, Massachusetts.

The canvas of this portrait is exceedingly thin. The canvases in the collection show considerable variation in thickness because of the different materials which artists used on which to paint. There is in the collection a portrait of a young man from Middlesex County. (Page 19.) Whatever was the material used for the portrait, it was so thin that you could almost see through it, and time had made it very brittle so that it had to be carefully lined in order to preserve it. The material appeared to be part of an old sheet, and a badly worn one at that. Fortunately, it was possible to preserve it. The young man in this portrait is very picturesque. He has on a black

[189]

velvet coat, a white satin vest on which falls a lace fichu, with a high collar and stock. He sits in a red chair on which his hand rests holding a letter. There is some writing on the letter. The other hand is thrust into his waistcoat. His hair is fuzzy and looks as if it had been pulled into a cue.

But if this portrait was painted on a thin cotton sheet, it is nothing to compare with that of Hannah Holmes of Howland, Maine, which was painted on brown paper. (Page 222.) The paint was put on very thick and, strangely enough, it has weathered the stress of years. But this material, too, had to be lined in order to preserve it. The portrait was painted by Albert Gallatin Hoit in 1833.

A letter received from a lady in Mattapoisett, Massachusetts, says: 'In 1831 my grandfather and my grandmother had their portraits painted by this artist, A. G. Hoit. Now from what was told me as a child, I will tell you of the artist. He came to Bangor and painted all the important people, apparently, and then went on to my grandfather's up the River to Howland, where he stayed long enough to paint my grandparents and a cousin visiting there.' (This cousin was the young woman whose portrait has just been described.) 'I am not sure whether the artist intended coming back to finish it, or rather make a portrait on canvas before he went abroad, or whether this cousin of my grandmother's died almost immediately of quick consumption. She did die up there in Howland and is buried in the old family plot.'

A portrait that it is well to mention here is that of the wife of a major of note from Bennington, Vermont, probably Major Hanks. (Page 169.) We should like to think so. It is quite unique in its way, for the lady was evidently a very prominent person and well-to-do. Her velvet dress looks as though it belonged to her: the beautiful lace bertha she wears naturally, and it seems to befit her, as does the cameo brooch which she wears on her breast. Around her neck is twined a heavy gold chain which falls below her waistline; at the end of it is an elaborate golden key, as was the fashion then. A diamond ring is on her forefinger, and her wedding ring with its guard ring of gold is on her fourth finger. She holds a book in her hand, which instead of being the usual red color, as seemed to be essential in the portraits of that day, is made of yellow parchment. She has long gold earrings falling from her ears, and her black hair is plastered to her head, except for the ringlets that fall on each side of her face. These were the kind that were brushed onto a wooden curling-stick, being stiff and uncompromising. She sits in the usual red chair. Her face is highly colored like those of the Wood girls.

This reminds me that when a certain member of the American Antiquarian Society of Worcester was carefully examining this picture, he told me that he was persuaded that it was painted by the same artist who painted Miss Wood and her sister of Townsend, Massachusetts; he proceeded to point out to me that the backgrounds were precisely similar in color and technique, that the paint was put on in the same manner, that the faces had the same doll-like expressions, and many other points of similarity, so that I began to think it must be so. The fact that the so-called Wood sisters were painted in Massachusetts and the wife of Major X in Vermont has no bearing on the subject, for the itinerant portrait painters roamed far afield through many states. This portrait of the Major's wife is a much more pretentious one than the other two. It commands attention.

The buckle worn at the waistline, which is to be found in so many of these portraits, marks a certain period, one might almost say the very year in which the portrait was painted, this being between 1838 and 1845. There was also a fashion which can be seen demonstrated in this collection of those who wear the long gold chain with a watch key on the end. These keys were sometimes very elaborately made, and were often like a jewel in themselves. The portrait of the wife of Major X from Vermont shows one of these.

The portrait of Obadiah Sampson (page 202) by Noah Alden, painted in 1830, is a rough but strong portrait. It is perfectly simple, just the plain portrait of a man with no frills. But the face has great personality and is vigorously portrayed. Sampson wears a rather ill-fitting black coat and white collar, but he has dignity for all that.

There are two other portraits in the collection by Noah Alden. (Pages 203 and 204.) They are of Jeremiah Kelley and his wife, Sarah C. Kelley, and were painted in 1830. These have the same vigorous quality that is evident in the portrait of Obadiah Sampson. Sarah is painted seated in a red chair which is close to a grey stone pillar, which forms a part of the background. The other half is sky. She wears a black dress, and across her shoulders is a thin, transparent scarf of greyish white. The neck is cut low and edged with a lace frill. The cap is of coarse lace with a bright blue ribbon folded around the crown, leaving a deep frill around her face, which is more or less young and rather pretty; the ribbon is tied in a bow under her chin. Her hair is light and she wears it with two fat puffs on either side of her brow. Her face is florid, and out from it look two blue eyes that match the ribbons on her cap. In her hand she holds the proverbial red book.

Jeremiah Kelley has a red curtain behind him as a background, the rest of which depicts sky and mountains. He is seated, wearing a black coat, white waistcoat, collar, and stock. He holds a book with a brown cover of calfskin in his hand. He has the same ruddy face that Obadiah Sampson has, and heavy black eyebrows. The portrait is strongly painted and is a typical Noah Alden one. This artist came from Middleboro, Massachusetts.

I will mention here the work of William Thompson Bartoll, for he was a very popular painter in those days. There are three portraits of his in the Fruitlands picture gallery. (Pages 223, 224, and 225.) They are of Mrs. Bessom and her husband, Mr. Bessom, also one of Sarah Fabyan West, wife of Josiah

West of Salem, Massachusetts. These are considerably beyond the work of the usual itinerant portrait painter. They are really fine portraits.

William Thompson Bartoll was born in 1817 and baptized in Marblehead, Massachusetts. He was the son of John and Rebecca Bartoll. He married Sally Selman in 1835. There are a number of his portraits now hanging in the public library at Marblehead.

What I consider to be one of the most interesting portraits of the collection is that of a little lady from Essex County, Massachusetts, because she is absolutely typical of the old New England towns in that county. I am quite sure that anybody looking at this portrait (page 226) would say that he had seen dozens of women like her, though the type has almost disappeared now. I call the portrait 'Aunt Lucinda,' for I feel sure that was the name she must have gone by. She has a little sallow face with deep lines in it, and out from behind a large pair of spectacles her eyes shine like gimlets. She has hair of no particular color — drab might express it better than anything else — and on it she wears an apology for a little cap made of black and lavender lace. Her dress is black, absolutely plain, and just showing the edge of a white collar around her throat. No one could see her without feeling sure that she sampled every unique patent medicine and cure-all that was launched each year on the market. I am sure that she partook freely of pickled limes with every meal, followed by frequent doses of Jamaica ginger. Little women of this type are always interesting to the listener, for they talk wisely though incessantly. I am sure she had a cure for everything, and would tell you what you should have done under circumstances which you could not possibly bring back.

Even in the most isolated country districts this type is to be found so few and far between now that it has become almost extinct — more is the pity.

Another portrait, of a young gentleman this time, is one

that came from Newburyport, Massachusetts. (Page 227.) There is something very attractive about him. He has a fresh, florid face that looks as if the sea breezes had played upon it. He wears a black coat and a collar and stock. This portrait was painted by Lyman Emerson Cole or Charles Octavius Cole. The Coles, root and branch, were artists, from Thomas Cole, the landscape painter, down. They all painted well. It was a very interesting clan. This portrait was painted about 1839.

I must mention here a portrait (page 228) of I. B. Wetherbee of Warren, Maine, painted by R. McFarlane in 1843. Whether this young man was closely related to the artist Wetherbee I do not yet know, but he died young. He is of a type that was to be found in New England, the kind that lead a more or less secluded life, and was a dreamer and loved nature, but could not do much else. Many of that type joined the Shakers and the Millerites and found peace amongst those highly sensitive organizations. His pale face is ornamented with a straggly chin beard, which was thin by nature, as though he were not vigorous enough to put forth a full growth. He has on a black suit of clothes which was evidently his 'Sunday best.' This is the only portrait of R. McFarlane's that I have come across, and it is rather a good one. It was presented to the collection by C. E. Merrill of Newton, Massachusetts.

Another portrait (page 229) of an earlier date is that of Mr. Andrew Fuller of Lancaster, Massachusetts. He is dressed in his military uniform, a blue coat with brass buttons, white shirt and stock, and his light hair brushed up and standing erect upon his head. The background of this portrait is a combination of the colors red, white, and blue, evidently as a suggestion of the stars and stripes. He is a very good-looking young man and makes an attractive picture. He is the ancestor of the well-known Fuller family of Lancaster.

The portrait (page 230) of Mrs. Ayer of Salem, Massachusetts, is to my mind one of the best in the collection, though, unfortunately, the artist is unknown. There is a warmth and depth to the texture of the black velvet dress, and a delicacy to the collar from Fayal, and the lace sides of her small cap which is tied under the chin, that command admiration and respect. She wears glasses though she is a young woman. They do not detract from the charm of her face. Her hair is blonde with a lovely sheen on it. And what is unusual in this portrait is that the hands are shapely and well painted. It must have been painted by some artist of note, if we could only know who it was.

One portrait (page 231) that always appeals to the public is that of an old lady knitting, found in Essex County, Massachusetts. She sits in a carved wooden chair very comfortably, with a red curtain as a background. Her face is full of furrows that tell of a life of work, and anxious days and happy days, and days of long routine. A little cap rests upon her head made of black velvet ribbon and grey lace. Her hair is streaked with grey. So as to keep warm, she wears a dark woollen jacket over her grey dress. The ribbons from her cap are tied under her chin. She holds her knitting in her hand. It is a sock done on three needles, and she is busily at work. The artist is unknown.

People stand before the picture and say, 'Oh, isn't she a dear old lady! She makes me think of my grandmother,' and then they begin to reminisce.

I found a rather unique picture (page 232) in Pepperell, Massachusetts, of a young girl playing an accordion. It was evidently the intention of the artist to bring her many talents and interests to the fore. She stands erect holding the accordion in her hands with her fingers on the keys. On a table near-by there is a pile of books. Right behind her is a table with a vase on it, with the word 'Remembrance' written upon it. It would seem that it was put there from a sentiment of which the public cannot know. There are fluted stone pillars in the background and a red curtain. The girl wears a grey-blue dress, cut somewhat low in the neck with box-plaited ribbon of a lighter shade of grey edging it, the ends of which fall down upon the breast. A strip of white muslin edged with lace covers the front part of her neck. Her brown hair, evidently curled over the old-fashioned curling-sticks, hangs in bunches on either side of her face.

The detail in this picture is worthy of a Dutch artist. The drawing is good and the paint and coloring are clear. It is a strange picture, but it is unusual and interesting. The artist is unknown. This of course is a real primitive.

PORTRAIT OF A LADY IN A GREEN DRESS FROM BOSTON,
MASSACHUSETTS
Painted by Philip Hewins in 1835.
(Description, pages 182, 183)

PORTRAIT OF MISS WYMAN OF WINCHENDON, MASSACHUSETTS
Painted by Dobson in 1845.
(Description, pages 183, 184)

[198]

PORTRAIT OF HELEN BRADBURY OF BUXTON, MAINE
Artist unknown.
(Description, page 185)

PORTRAIT OF MRS. O. E. S. FRINCK OF MEDFORD,
MASSACHUSETTS
Painted by her husband.
(Description, page 188)

PORTRAIT OF THE DAUGHTER OF THE LIGHTHOUSE-KEEPER AT
OWL'S HEAD, MAINE

Artist unknown. Painted about 1845.
(Description, pages 188, 189)

[201]

PORTRAIT OF OBADIAH SAMPSON OF MASSACHUSETTS
Painted by Noah Alden in 1830.
(Description, page 192)

PORTRAIT OF JEREMIAH KELLEY
Painted by Noah Alden in 1830.
(Description, page 192)

PORTRAIT OF SARAH C. KELLEY
Painted by Noah Alden in 1830.
(Description, page 192)

CHAPTER VIII

O<small>NE</small> of the best and most popular painters around 1820 was Ethan Allen Greenwood. He was born in 1779 and died in 1856.

I received the following letter from his granddaughter in regard to him:

'Barre, October 4, 1938 — My grandfather began painting in 1801 when at Worcester Academy, and from then till 1825 he painted about five hundred portraits.... He would take his kit and go into families and paint all the members. He went to Dartmouth College in 1802, and while there went to New York and studied with Mr. Edward Savage, and after graduating from Dartmouth studied law, and was admitted to the bar in Worcester, all the time continuing his painting.

'As he painted in the different towns you mention, Pepperell, Winchendon, Westminster, and more than fifty other towns and cities, and among them Harvard, where in 1812 he painted Mr. and Mrs. Hayward, William Porter, Jaron Bigelow, and Edmund Foster, I thought possibly you might have some of these, or know if they are still in Harvard. He went to Boston to reside in June, 1812, the very day war was declared, and had rooms in the old Province House, which has been torn down quite recently.

'In the morning of July 4th, 1818, he attended with the Masons the laying of the cornerstone of the Massachusetts General Hospital, and that evening opened the New England Museum on the corner of Court and Market Streets (now Cornhill, I think), and he also had an Academy of Fine Arts on Market Street. He obtained permission to take the portraits of Governor Winthrop, Bradstreet, and others from the State House, to make còpies for his own collection.

'A few days ago, I saw your notice of "Please read this" in the newspaper and then decided to write you about my grandfather.

'Since the hurricane in 1939 I looked up his account of the one they had on September 23, 1815, when "trees were uprooted on Boston Common and the Mall, roofs blown off, etc., and it was a day of terror and desolation." He bought one of the buttonwood trees and tried to have it sawed on the Common, but they could not spare the time, so he had it drawn to Charlestown to the sawmill!

'Just below this account was the following: "October 1, 1815, evening at Dow's (a store, I imagine). My picture of Mr. Dow together with Cole's paintings had been there for several days under the ordeal of criticism, and mine had gained the preference, and I was glad of that, for I was reluctant to putting myself on trial with Cole, but as it was a plan of his own, I had no objection to beating him." I expect that this was the J. G. Cole, 1826, that was listed in your article.

'You asked for incidents. Of course, there were many. One that amused me was about people in a Vermont town, who, like others, have their peculiarities; for instance, "Offer your hand to a gentleman, and he will present three fingers, the first finger and thumb being always occupied with a large pinch of snuff."

'Mr. Greenwood was my grandmother's second husband, but the only father she knew, as her father died when she was only three years old.

'He was born in Hubbardston in 1779 and died in 1856, and I was only six years old, but I remember him perfectly with his ruffled shirt and yellow broadcloth vest. I shall be interested to know if you have any portraits with his signature that are unknown to you. If you had the date and residence I might be able to help you to identify them.

'Cordially yours,'

As it happens, I did have two beautiful portraits by Greenwood. (Pages 263 and 264.) They are of Mr. and Mrs. Francis Amory. These portraits were painted in 1813. Mr. Francis Amory was a Boston man. The background of his portrait is of dark greenish-grey. He has brown curly hair brushed to the front, as was the fashion around 1800. He wears a black coat, white vest, a high winged collar with stock, and a frilly lace jabot and soft white tie. He is an exceedingly good-looking man, and the picture makes the most of it.

His wife, Mrs. Francis Amory, also has a greenish-grey background in her portrait. She has brown eyes, her complexion is fair and peach-like, and her pretty blonde hair is curled about her face, held in by a black velvet band, which is tied around the head. Her long hair was wound in a braid like a crown. She has long pendant pearl earrings, and a bright red silk shawl is draped over one shoulder. Her white dress is made in the Empire style, with the waist directly underneath the bust. A sheer lace covers her neck, and down the V-shaped front and around her throat is a box-plaited ruffle of exquisite lace, through which is twined a narrow greenish-blue ribbon, which falls in bows down the front.

Ethan Allen Greenwood signed his name and the date on Mrs. Amory's portrait, but not on that of her husband, as was the habit of that day. It does not seem ever to have occurred to these artists that two portraits of a married couple in a family could be separated. I have found a number of these cases. Sometimes the husband's portrait has been signed, in which case the wife's portrait has not been signed, and vice versa.

The lady from whom these were procured had inherited

them from her father who was adopted by the daughter of
Francis Amory. They hung for years in a house on Chambers
Street, which is the first street before you come to the Harrison
Gray Otis House on Cambridge Street, Boston. At the time
these portraits were painted, that was a very fashionable
quarter of Boston. The Harrison Gray Otis House was one of
the most beautiful in the city of Boston. It is now the head-
quarters of the Society for the Preservation of New England
Antiquities.

These two portraits are exceptionally lovely. The remark
is frequently made by visitors to the gallery that they might
easily have been painted by Gilbert Stuart.

Two other portraits (pages 253 and 254) of interest are
those of Doctor Henry Kittredge and his wife Naomi (Pink-
erton-Brown) Kittredge of Tewksbury, Massachusetts. These
were painted by Sanford Mason in 1838. The background of
his portrait is of greyish-green, and he sits in a tapestry up-
holstered chair. He has curly black hair and a black coat,
white vest, and a high collar, which almost covers his chin,
around which is wound a black satin cravat.

Mrs. Naomi Kittredge is depicted as a handsome woman
with sparkling black eyes and brilliant coloring. Her black
hair is curled all over her head and gathered into a big knot
on one side. She has on a low-cut black dress, and over one
shoulder is draped a brilliant red silk shawl. Naomi was
evidently a dashing type of woman, if one can tell by her portrait, but both these specimens are exceedingly well painted,
and both are agreeable to look upon.

The portrait painter, William Sanford Mason, is listed in
the *Dictionary of American Painters, Sculptors, and Engravers* as a
painter and an engraver. He did a great deal of work throughout Massachusetts, and then went to Philadelphia, where he
was working about 1865. He made several copies of 'The
Washington Family at Mount Vernon' after the painting of
Savage.

All portraits by Joseph Greenleaf Cole have atmosphere and an element of romance in them. I received a letter on March 20, 1940, from a lady who wrote me about a picture she owned of her great-grandfather and also her grandfather. She describes how the former was dressed, and writes of him thus:

'He was stern of eye, narrow of lip, every bit the Puritan and the military man. Evidently his daughters would fain escape from too much discipline, for Grandfather Dill, seated on a bluish-green armless chair, is all the romantic, idealistic type; round-eyed, visionary, a full-lipped expressive person. He wears a black suit with a white shirt-front surmounted by a standing collar slightly turned over, a black stock swathed about his neck and knotted in front. Maybe that Mary Paul (his wife) married this thoroughly nice young man even as her sister became the wife of Joseph Jefferson, the actor. The girls evidently did not at all care for the continuance of disciplinary traits.'

This describes this portrait (page 260) and the young man very well. As she wrote, he was the romantic, idealistic type.

We have a very interesting example here showing the change that came over some of these artists after having been itinerants and emerged again, taking their place in the ranks of ripened and popular portrait painters. This is what happened to Albert Gallatin Hoit.

In Chapter VII we saw his portrait of Susan Pierce Jarvis, painted in 1830, the period of his itinerant days. After that he had gathered sufficient funds to enable him to set sail for France and Italy, and he studied there under several masters.

Now comes his portrait of John Belcher Callender. (Page 256.) Here one notices the European influence and the surer technique. The style is more romantic. This portrait was painted twelve years later, in 1842. It depicts a lovely background of rolling hills, woods, blue sky with clouds shading the valley. The boy is sitting on a terrace with his back against an ornamental stone pillar surmounted by a stone vase. He has on a black velvet coat, white and rather baggy trousers, black shoes and white stockings. He has beautiful curls that are glossy and brown and evidently curled over the old-fashioned curling-stick. His eyes are brown and match his hair. He wears a white frilled collar falling loosely enough to show his throat. A Springer spaniel is crouched beside him, and is looking up at him eagerly, with adoring eyes, and showing a bit of his red tongue. A leather collar is around the dog's neck with a blue ribbon tied to it, one end of which is held in the boy's hand. The other end falls down upon his white trousers. Almost behind the stone pillar falls a red curtain, edged with a yellow satin border. There is imagination and poetry in the picture, probably the result of the artist's sojourn in Italy.

The same transformation is noticeable in the painting of Joseph Greenleaf Cole. In Chapter VI is a portrait of Captain Greeley by this same artist painted in 1826 in his days of itinerancy. He evidently was one of the thrifty artists who knew how to save his pennies, which enabled him to go to Boston and paint in a wider field. The only mention of instruction that is given in the accounts of his life is that which he received after this from his father, Moses Cole of Newburyport, who was also an artist. This started him on a new standard, of which the portrait of Mary Hersey Callender is an example. (Page 257.) This was painted in 1845, and shows the maturing and definite effects of the instruction Hoit had received. In this picture the background is a cloudy sky melting into a reddish sunset. The child sits on a rock on the side of a hill with the slope of the mountain back of her, and at the extreme left of the picture is a tiny glimpse of the sea, dark blue in color. She is leaning on a huge black Newfoundland dog, with great seeing eyes and a white band around his nose. Mary has straight brown hair and brown eyes. She wears a brilliant cherry-red dress, low-neck, with white muslin edging. She has on white muslin pantalettes with two rows of drawn work on each leg. On her feet are little black shoes and wrinkled white socks, while beside her lies her hat, a big yellow straw with blue ribbons. There is green grass growing on the top of the rock on which she and the dog sit. On the extreme right lies a closed pink lily, with green spiked leaves, which has evidently just been picked and carelessly laid there. The portrait is painted with strength and vigor, and shows how the hidden talent when given the chance rose to the surface.

Another portrait (page 255) by the same artist, Joseph Greenleaf Cole, painted in 1840, is of Sarah Elizabeth Hersey Ashton Callender, who was the first wife of Benjamin Callender, and the mother of the two children above by Cole and Hoit. She was born in 1816 and died young, at the age of thirty-two. The portrait has a dark background with an oval in the centre over which trails a green vine. Within this oval sits the lady with coal-black hair and appealing dark eyes. She has a thoughtful, sensitive face and a delicate throat rising from a lovely neck and shoulders.

She wears a low-cut glorious red velvet dress, cut V-shaped in front to the waist and laced across with silk lacing over white gauze. Her left arm, over which hangs an Oriental shawl, rests upon the oval, and the hand drops over it holding a small bunch of flowers. There is a broad gold bracelet on the wrist. Unlike many of the portraits of the time, the hair is done with the greatest simplicity. It is parted in the middle and smoothed down on the side of the head as far as the ear.

On pages 258 and 259 are shown the portraits of Benjamin Callender, her husband, and his second wife, painted about 1850.

With the various portraits in this collection by Joseph Greenleaf Cole, there is an opportunity to notice the ever-rising standard of his paintings. By the time he painted members of the Callender family he had reached his high-water mark, and was greatly considered as a portrait painter. To take note of the progress of the individual work of these itinerant portrait painters who began on the first rung of the ladder and climbed upwards is a most fascinating study. It shows the grit and verve that possessed them, and that is one of the reasons why their work is more honest and true to nature than that of many of the artists who had others to lean upon.

An interesting portrait (page 261) and an early one of an ancestor of a very prominent family in Boston is that of Anna (Phillips) Shaw, who was born on November 29, 1756, and was married to Mr. Samuel Shaw in 1792 by the Reverend Joseph Erkley of Boston. Mrs. Shaw is dressed according to the George Washington period. Her white hair is built out, making a large halo around her head, and a string of pearls formed in a circle rests upon it. Her dress is of a crushed pink, very delicate in color. She is not a good-looking woman — on the contrary there is something weather-beaten about her face, but the picture as a whole reminds one of the work of the artist Greuze. It is painted as though it were a pastel. It came from the Dorothy Quincy Nourse Estate.

There are two portraits (pages 235 and 236) which also go back to an earlier date, those of Mr. and Mrs. Moses Thayer of Boston (Mrs. Thayer was a Miss Sargent). They are exceedingly well painted. Mr. Thayer was a very good-looking man, and shows off well his black coat and yellow satin waistcoat, topped by the high collar and white stock. He has dark brown hair and a very fresh complexion.

Mrs. Thayer is dressed in a green dress in a style of the First Empire. There are lace ruffles about the low-cut neck, puffed sleeves, and thin, tight undersleeves, made of gauze and clinging closely to the arm. A necklace of blue-green stones with a heart-shaped stone hanging from it falls from the neck. She wears a lace bow on top of her hair, which is curled about the face. She is evidently quite a little older than Mr. Thayer.

There is nothing on the portraits to reveal who the artist was who painted them, which seems a pity.

The portrait of a lady came out of an old Beacon Hill house in Boston. (Page 262.) It was painted by Cephas Giovanni Thompson around 1850.

Cephas Giovanni Thompson was born in Middleboro, Massachusetts. He began painting portraits in Plymouth at the age of nineteen and worked his way to Boston, Bristol, Providence, and Philadelphia. He then went to New York City and remained there from 1837 to 1847. He next went to New Bedford and painted some forty portraits there, and then to Boston, where he was in great demand, being one of those who was very evidently climbing the rungs of the ladder very fast. Having collected enough funds, he went to Europe in 1852 and visited London, Paris, Florence, and Rome, where he remained for seven years. When he returned, he stopped in New York City and was fortunate enough to have a great deal of work to do there.

In the book, *Artists of the Nineteenth Century and Their Works*, by Clement and Hutton, we find the following item:

> Mr. Thompson's works are known throughout America, and many specimens were in England, France, Russia, etc. Before going to Europe, he painted a series of American authors, including Hoffman (belonging to the New York Historical Society), Dr. Francis, and others. His portrait of Hawthorne, with whom, while in Italy, he was on intimate terms, was engraved, and is in the edition of 'Twice Told Tales,' published by Ticknor and Fields. His full-length portrait of Dr. Mathews, the first president of the New York University, is in the President's room of that Institution. A notice in the 'Richmond Inquirer' says, in speaking of one of his noted pictures (Saint Peter led from the Prison by an Angel), 'It is certainly a beautiful picture, full of genius and spirit.'

The artist Jarvis in an article written in *Art Idea* says:

> None of our artists has brought back with him from Italy a

more thorough knowledge and appreciation of the old masters, technically, historically or authentically, than Cephas G. Thompson. He conscientiously endeavors to infuse their lofty feelings and motives into his own refined manner.

Nathaniel Hawthorne, whose portrait Thompson painted, speaks of him in *The Marble Faun* regarding his pictures of 'Prospero and Miranda,' and 'Saint Peter led from the Prison by an Angel,' as follows:

> ... Or we might bow before an artist who has wrought too sincerely, too religiously, with too earnest feeling, and too delicate a touch, for the world at once to recognize how much toil and thought are compressed into the stately brow of Prospero and Miranda's maids in loveliness, or from what a depth within this painter's heart the Angel is leading forth Saint Peter.

On March 11, 1858, we find this in Hawthorne's diary:

> Via Porta, Palazzo Larazani. Today we called at Mr. Thompson's studio, and he had on the easel a little picture of St. Peter released from prison by the angels, which I saw once before. It is very beautiful indeed, and deeply and spiritually conceived, and I wish I could afford to have it finished for myself. ... I do not think there is a better painter than Mr. Thompson living, among the Americans at least, not one so earnest, faithful, and religious in his worship of art. I would rather look at his pictures than at any except the very finest of the Old Masters, and, taking into consideration only the comparative pleasure to be derived, I would not accept more than one or two of those. In painting, as in literature, I suspect there is something in the productions of the day that takes the fancy more than the works of any past age — not greater merit nor nearly so great, but better suited to this very present time.
>
> Mr. Thompson is a true artist, and whatever his pictures have of beauty comes from very far beneath the surface; and this I suppose, is one weighty reason why he has but moderate success. I should like his pictures for mere color, even if they represented nothing. His studio is in the Via Sistina; and at a little

distance on the other side of the same street, is William Story's, where we likewise went, and found him at work on a sitting statue of Cleopatra.

Arnold's *Art and Artists in Rhode Island* speaks of Thompson in this way: 'He was a handsome little man with an engaging smile. Praised by Hawthorne whose portrait he painted.'

The delightful portrait of two children (page 233) was painted by Alexander Hamilton Emmons, born in 1816 in East Haddam, Connecticut. The greatest number of his portraits and miniatures were painted in Hartford and Norwich.

> When he was a boy in school he held the reputation of being the picture-maker of the district. Necessity compelled him to learn the trade of a house-painter. A portrait which he made of a fellow laborer opened his eyes to the fact that he might be a portrait painter. He began at once painting miniature portraits on Bristol-board. When twenty years old he married, and, being the only artist in Norwich, found instantly sufficient orders for support, regardless of the fact that the pictures were his first experiments. In 1843 he opened a studio in Hartford.... His only absence of any length was during an extended trip through Europe for the purpose of studying the work of the old masters. His work showed great improvement in refinement, taste, and general execution, after his return.
>
> Mr. Emmons' native talent was obvious in all his work, much of which was remarkable for a man who never had an instructor beyond his own observation.

The portrait of the lady with the beautiful Fayal collar follows that of the two children. (Page 234.) She was their grandmother.

CHAPTER IX

I WILL now quote at length from William Dunlap's *The History of the Arts of Design in the United States* in regard to Francis Alexander and James Frothingham, because he gives the results of personal interviews with these two artists, having been a contemporary of theirs, and no amount of searching could uncover such details as he was able to record of the lives of these two men.

I will start with Francis Alexander. He was born in Killingsby, Windham County, Connecticut, on the 3d of February, 1800. Very fortunately, he gave an account of his life to Dunlap, an artist of that period, and I will quote from that account.

His father was a farmer of moderate circumstances, and he says that his course in early life was none of the smoothest,

> it being midst rocks and stumps, briers and thistles, and finally through all the perplexities and privations incident to the life of a poor farmer's son. I might tell you of going barefooted to church hundreds of times in warm weather three miles distant, and of a thousand similar incidents, such as would only convince you of early poverty after all. From the age of eight up to twenty, I labored almost incessantly, the eight warm months of the year upon my father's farm. The other four months of the year I went to a country district school till I was seventeen. My eighteenth and nineteenth winters I kept school and taught the small fry under my charge the bad pronunciation and bad reading which I had imbibed from my old schoolmasters, and which I have found it so difficult to unlearn since. I had never received any pay whatever for services upon the farm, except food, cloth-

ing and schooling, so you may well guess that the forty dollars which I received from school keeping formed a pile in my eye more majestic than an Egyptian pyramid. The next winter I received forty-four dollars for the same time in the same district. The summer intervening, I labored upon the farm, and the summer following till August; during that month loss of bodily strength owing to the severe labor of haying and reaping obliged me to hang up my scythe and sickle, and take to the house. I was only comfortably ill however, and for diversion I went out in the boat fishing upon the pond, the beautiful pond, which helps to make the scenery about my father's house so very picturesque.

Well, I caught a pickerel, some perch and roach. While I was idly gazing upon their beautiful tints and fine forms, it occurred to me that they would look very pretty painted, and I thought of a box of water colors which had been left me by a boy, and I went immediately home with the determination of painting the fish. I laid them on the table, hunted up one solitary camel's hair pencil which had been given to me the year before, and went to copying nature for the first time. . . . I was delighted with the pictures. I thought then, and know now, that they were more like real objects than any paintings I had then seen. The family praised them, and an old fisherman who happened to see them said, if the painted fish were cut out of paper and laid upon the floor with real fish, that he should mistake the shadow for the reality! I, who had never received so much praise before, attempted other objects from nature, such as real flowers, dead birds, etc., with about the same success as before. I then made up my mind to become an ornamental or sign painter, merely because I thought I could make more money than by farming. My ambition rose no higher, indeed, my reading had been so limited and my birth so obscure, that I thought sign painting the highest branch of painting in the world. I had been to Providence, had seen signs there, and those were the only marvels in painting that I saw until I was twenty, excepting two ordinary portraits that I had seen at some country inn.

He made up his mind to go to New York and learn to

paint.... His friends all remonstrated with him, and his brothers said that he had better go into the field to work, and they all talked of laziness and a thousand other things in order to laugh him out of it. They even called it a wild project as a last resort of idleness to get rid of work, etc., but he was a determined young man and went against the advice of all of his friends and acquaintances.

He told of the vicissitudes of that visit to New York, and how his little stock of money began to dwindle, but he came across an artist named Robertson who took him into his school out of pity, and gave him a few things to copy in pencil and India ink. Finally at his particular request the artist let him copy some simple thing like a mountain or a lake, but he was not willing to remain so low down in the scale, and wanted to attempt something more difficult, but Robertson refused, and said he could not be allowed to copy heads or figures until he had been with him a number of months; so, of necessity, Alexander left him after staying five or six weeks with him. His money was all gone, and he barely had enough to get home with.

This was certainly disheartening, but his temperament was such as could not be discouraged and he made another attempt, and again went to New York by way of Norwich and New London. 'I took a deck passage on board the "Fulton" with Captain Law,' he wrote, 'who told me that I should be set down to New York for four dollars. I lodged on the cold deck in September without blanket or cloak. The "Fulton" in those days exchanged passengers at New Haven with the "Connecticut," Captain Bunker.'

Apparently this was too much for his pocketbook, as the charge was seven dollars before he even reached New York. The sum, he says, 'was more important to me than three hundred now.'

He returned to artist Robertson's school of painting again, and he says of it:

I had free access to the Academy over the school. That was a field of wonder to me, and what I saw there induced me afterwards to try my hand at painting heads or portraits. However, as I knew nothing of them, I began after my return home to ornament the plaster walls of one of the rooms in my father's house with rude landscapes introducing horses, sheep, hogs, hens and chickens, etc. Those who saw my productions looked astonished, but no farmer had taste enough to have his walls painted in the same way; I waited for patronage in landscape, but not having it, I determined to try my hand at portraits, so I shut my self up in the room I had just painted from top to bottom, and painted the head and shoulders of a man from fancy; I did not care who it resembled, I only strove to apply the shadows about the eyes, the nose and the mouth so as to produce the effect of those I had seen in the Academy in New York. I painted away, and began to be pleased with my work, as I advanced, and whistled in time with my feelings. My aged mother hearing me, came and knocked at the door, and said, 'You are successful, my son, I know by your whistling.' I seldom paint a portrait or anything else nowadays without thinking of the kind voice of my mother on that occasion; It was the first word I had heard uttered to encourage me onward in my new pursuit.

I finished the head and drapery all at one sitting, and then exhibited my work to my family. They seemed surprised, and all of them began to speak kindly to me.... The neighbors met the same evening at the schoolhouse, half a dozen of them, perhaps to talk of hiring a master... so I went to the schoolhouse with the picture in my hand. The neighbors were thunderstruck, they praised it and gazed at it till the business of the meeting was well nigh forgot. My brother William gazed steadily at it for at least half an hour without speaking. At length he exclaimed, 'Well Frank, if you paint ten years, you will not paint another so good as that.' They all praised it till I really thought I had done something wonderful. The next day, I called in a nephew of three years of age, and while he leaned upon my knee and played about me, I painted his portrait and finished it all at one standing. The day following I took the portrait of another nephew, six years old, and I represented him laughing, and showing his white rows of teeth. The portraits of my nephews were called excellent likenesses. My fame had now spread half a mile in one direction. I was offered five dollars by a Mr. Mason to paint a little Miss full length. I painted her and they all said it was a hit. Then the girl's mother offered me a dollar a day to come and paint the rest of the family, half a dozen of them. I went, and received thirteen dollars for thirteen days! My fame had now traveled several miles. I was invited to Thompson, to paint several families, and received three dollars a head and my board. As soon as I had received fifty or sixty dollars, I returned to New York for instruction in portrait painting, but I could not obtain it.

He then tells how a Mr. McKoy gave him Mr. Stuart's mode of setting the palette, and Colonel Trumbull lent him two heads to copy and treated him with much kindness. The artists Waldo and Jewett also lent him two portraits to copy. After copying them, and a few others, his funds were exhausted and he was forced to go back to Connecticut.

'On my return,' he writes, 'I had the boldness to ask eight dollars for a portrait, and received it. I was forced to travel, though, from town to town to find business.'

He then goes on to say that the widow of General James B. Mason sent to Killingsby for him to come to Providence and paint her family, promising him fifteen dollars a portrait. 'Accordingly I went,' he said, 'and was received into her family, where I remained five weeks, during which time I painted half a dozen. When I had finished two or three she took me into her chaise and drove all over Providence exhibiting them, and praising them to her numerous influential friends, and thus she prepared the public to receive me most graciously, as soon as I left her hospitable mansion.'

This same Mrs. Mason died while he was still in Providence, and he felt that he had lost one of his most valuable and disinterested friends.

PORTRAIT OF SUSAN PIERCE JARVIS OF CLAREMONT,
NEW HAMPSHIRE
Painted by Albert Gallatin Hoit in 1830.
(Description, pages 185, 186)

PORTRAIT OF HANNAH HOLMES OF HOWLAND, MAINE

Painted by Albert Gallatin Hoit in 1833. (*Painted on a piece of brown paper.*)

(Description, page 190)

PORTRAIT OF MR. BESSOM OF MARBLEHEAD, MASSACHUSETTS
Painted by William Thompson Bartoll in 1845.
(Description, page 192)

[223]

PORTRAIT OF MRS. BESSOM OF MARBLEHEAD, MASSACHUSETTS
Painted by William Thompson Bartoll in 1845.
(Description, pages 188, 192)

PORTRAIT OF SARAH FABYAN WEST, WIFE OF JOSIAH WEST OF
SALEM, MASSACHUSETTS
Painted by William Thompson Bartoll.
(Description, page 192)

[225]

PORTRAIT OF 'AUNT LUCINDA' OF ESSEX COUNTY,
MASSACHUSETTS
Artist unknown.
(Description, page 193)

[226]

PORTRAIT OF A YOUNG MAN FROM NEWBURYPORT,
MASSACHUSETTS

Painted by either Lyman Emerson Cole or Charles Octavius Cole about 1839.
(Description, pages 193, 194)

[227]

PORTRAIT OF I. B. WETHERBEE OF WARREN, MAINE
Painted by R. McFarlane in 1843.
(Description, page 194)

Portrait of Mr. Andrew Fuller of Lancaster,
Massachusetts
Artist unknown.
(Description, page 194)

[229]

PORTRAIT OF MRS. AYER, SALEM, MASSACHUSETTS
Artist unknown. Painted about 1840.
(Description, pages 194, 195)

PORTRAIT OF AN OLD LADY KNITTING, FROM ESSEX COUNTY,
MASSACHUSETTS

Artist unknown.

(Description, page 195)

PORTRAIT OF A GIRL WITH AN ACCORDION, FROM PEPPERELL,
MASSACHUSETTS
Artist unknown.
(Description, pages 195, 196)

[232]

PORTRAIT OF TWO CHILDREN
Painted by Alexander Hamilton Emmons in 1843.
(Description, page 215)

[233]

PORTRAIT OF THE GRANDMOTHER OF THE TWO CHILDREN
PAINTED BY ALEXANDER H. EMMONS IN 1843
Artist unknown.
(Description, page 215)

[234]

PORTRAIT OF MR. MOSES THAYER OF BOSTON, MASSACHUSETTS
Artist unknown.
(Description, page 212)

PORTRAIT OF MRS. MOSES (SARGENT) THAYER OF BOSTON,
MASSACHUSETTS
Artist unknown.
(Description, page 212)

'I painted two years or more in Providence,' he said, 'and received constant employ and from fifteen to twenty-five dollars for my portraits. I afterwards came to Boston, bringing a painting of two sisters with me, which I carried to Mr. Stuart for his opinion. I will give you his remarks. He said that they were very clever, and reminded him of the Gainsborough pictures, that I lacked many things that might be acquired by practice and study, but I had "that" which could not be acquired.'

Francis Alexander was a young man of the greatest possible perseverance. He tried to work out some profession for himself to gain the much-needed dollar, but even from a boy art was his secret ambition. He tried several mediums to reach this goal. At one time it was water-color, at another pastels, and finally oils. An artist named Alexander Robertson in New York gave him a few lessons in water-colors. He tried that for a while, but it did not satisfy him. He wanted to paint in oils above all things, so he went to Providence armed with optimism in search of patrons, but that did not seem to work out very well, so he went to Boston and opened a studio there. It was a distinct venture, but he managed to get sitters, and to give satisfaction. This gave him great encouragement.

It was on a fortunate day that he was introduced to Daniel Webster. The latter started the young man's career most effectually by letting him paint several portraits of himself which turned out to be excellent pieces of work. This was the beginning of his success. That fortune should have played such a trump card into his hands was almost startling, and people began to take note of this heretofore unknown artist who was suddenly coming into the limelight. He was the type of young man who left no stone unturned when he wanted to reach his goal, so while in Boston he managed to get to be known by Gilbert Stuart with the assistance of John Trumbull, to whom he had been introduced. Stuart at once took an interest in him, and helped him in a great many ways, and under his influence young Alexander advanced rapidly. His painting became more sure and vital. His whole mind was focussed on getting all that he could out of such an important friendship.

The early days of struggling seemed to him like a dream, but it was not a very long while before he began wishing to penetrate new horizons, and he set sail for Italy in 1831 in search of new inspiration, determined to perfect his talent of which he now realized that he was endowed. Italy proved to be all that he had hoped to find, but he could not remain there too long. On his return he painted portraits of Charles Dickens, Benjamin R. Curtis, John Odin, Baron Stow, Mrs. Fletcher Webster, and Mrs. Thomas Gray with her son, Gorham Gray, a beautiful portrait (page 266) which is in the picture gallery at Harvard, Massachusetts, and many others. The list is a long one.

He was a man of endless perseverance and turned his talents in many directions. He drew on stone, the earliest attempts at portrait lithography in America, which gives an idea of his versatility. He was one of the very few artists who stopped his career while he was at the very height of it. He died in 1846.

Mrs. Thomas Gray's portrait is a very beautiful one. She certainly helped it by being a very lovely woman. She is dressed in a black velvet dress, with an embroidered muslin collar, amply ruffled, over which hangs a black velvet cloak trimmed with brown fur (possibly sable). The cloak falls off the shoulders somewhat, revealing the graceful lines of her figure. She wears a very small and becoming muslin cap trimmed with light blue flowers embroidered on it. A narrow blue ribbon is tied under her chin to hold it on. Her brown hair is soft and wavy, and matches her brown eyes.

Her little son, Gorham Gray, stands by her knee. He has light hair with ringlets falling on each side of his face, and beautiful blue eyes and pink cheeks. He wears a grey dress with a full skirt, and holds an open book with a red cover. As has been explained in an earlier chapter, small boys were dressed like girls up to a certain age during that period, hence the curls and the grey skirt.

The two figures are beautifully modelled. Mrs. Gray is smiling. Her lips are parted, and behind them one gets a glimpse of her white teeth. The portrait is a most appealing one, and it shows what heights can be reached if a young man starts out having only the one intense desire and will-power to get to the top.

'In Boston,' he writes, 'I received forty dollars for the head and shoulders, twenty-five by thirty-inch canvas, and more according to the size. Two years afterwards I received fifty dollars, and seventy-five for the kit-cat size. These were the prices until I went away.'

Like all the artists of that period, he had no sooner acquired a certain amount of success than he began to long for Italy, and as he had been able to put aside quite a little money, he sailed for Genoa. He saw the fine paintings there and then went to Florence, where he renewed his acquaintance with Mr. Thomas Cole, the artist, and went with him to Rome. From there they took an ideal trip together to Naples, visited Herculaneum, Pompeii, and Paestum, and then returned to Rome. While in Rome, he wrote:

> I painted the portrait of Miss Harriet Douglas of New York. Sir Walter Scott being there at the time, an acquaintance of hers, came with Miss Douglas in her carriage to my studio, where he remained for nearly an hour, conversing all the while in a most familiar manner. I had painted an original Magdalen. It was standing on one side of the studio at the time, and Sir Walter moved his chair up within six feet of it. There he sat looking at it for several minutes without speaking. I was all impatience to know what he would say. He turned away with the laconic remark, 'she's been forgiven.' I returned to Florence, stayed a few weeks, went to Venice, stayed seven months; returned to

Rome the following winter, and stayed three months more; returned again to Florence and visited Bologna, Pisa, and Leghorn, thence to Paris, stayed twenty days; thence to London, there ten days only, left it in the London Packet for New York, and arrived in New York on the 25th of August or the 24th.

After visiting my friends a month or two, I took my old room again here in Boston (Columbian Hall) where I have commenced painting with success, received one hundred dollars for portraits; have not fixed upon prices yet for more than busts, choosing to recommend myself first, knowing that the good people of our good country are willing to pay according to merit.

Mr. Cole can perhaps give you some information about your humble servant if you desire more.

When I was a farmer I used to go three miles before sun rise to reap a bushel of rye per day, and return at night. Oh! had you seen me then, winding my way to my labors, shoeless, and clad in trousers and shirt of tow, with my sickle on my shoulder. As you are a painter you might have given me a few cents to sit for my picture.

Yours truly,

FRANCIS ALEXANDER

It can be said of James Frothingham that in 1834 he was one of our best portrait painters. He commenced the working business of life as a builder of chaise bodies, the trade his father followed and intended for him. He was born in Charlestown, Massachusetts, near Boston, in 1786. James early commenced attempts at drawing, and as he succeeded, to the admiration of his schoolmates, applause excited ambition. After a while he gained the art of chaise building. His first step towards the painting art was to color the chaise bodies made by himself and his father. In those days this mystery was imparted only by masters to their apprentices under the seal of secrecy, and the youth had to devise means by which to compel the colors to adhere to the wood, and to make one layer of paint keep its place over another. Many unsuccessful attempts did not discourage him, and he finally, notwithstanding the extreme closeness of the coach and chaise painters in the neighborhood, mastered the art.

In the meantime his experiments in drawing had been in progress, and from copying a print from a child's book, line by line, he had attained to the representation of a bowl, a cat, and other objects technically called still life, with an encouraging degree of truth. At this period of his progress towards his destined profession, someone suggested that portraits might be made with black and white chalk on grey paper. He tried with charcoal and chalk, and prevailed upon a relative to sit to him. This was pronounced a monstrous likeness. The next he sat to himself and produced a portrait in India ink. The portrait of his grandfather in oil colors was the next experiment. He had never seen a painter's palette, but contrived a machine for himself, such as he thought proper for the purpose. It was a piece of board, in which he made holes to receive as many thimbles as he had colors, which, diluted with oil, were thus disposed of, every thimble to its hole in the board, every color to its thimble ready to receive the brush. Of tints or mingling of colors he knew nothing. With this original apparatus, and without instruction, he commenced portrait painting, while yet applying himself to the discovery of some mode by which to accomplish chaise painting, at the same time working at his trade.

His mode of making out a likeness was as unusual as his palette was original. He painted first the forehead and finished it. Then one eye, and afterwards the other, finishing each as he went, and so, feature by feature, to the chin. The hair was then put on, the drapery followed, and last a background. Even thus working in the dark, he made such pictures as called forth the applause of his father's neighbors and his own associates.

That the lad should have been in the neighborhood of Boston all his life, and striving to paint from childhood, and yet have remained in total ignorance of the mode of operation adopted by others, is a curious fact. Of the fact I am assured by Mr. Frothingham himself. It marks a degree of seclusion from that portion of society to which all these matters are familiar, which at first sight appears very strange; but perhaps we should find in the occupation of the father and the associates of the young man a sufficient explanation. So far, Frothingham had been almost self-taught.

Having been sent on business to Lancaster, Massachusetts, he there met with his first portrait painter, Mr. Whiting. He was the son of General Whiting, an old Revolutionary soldier. This gentleman did not continue long in the profession, but entered the Army of the United States. At this time, however, he had the power and the will to show young Frothingham what kind of instrument a painter's palette was, and how painters used it. Mr. Whiting had sought and received instruction from Stuart. He communicated freely what he had freely received, and Frothingham was told with what colors the great painter set his palette, how he mingled his tints, and in some measure how he used them.

The youth returned home elated with his acquired knowledge, and eager to put in practice the lessons he had received. He procured a palette, dismissed his thimbles, procured colors and oils as directed, and began a portrait in the usual manner as he had been instructed by Whiting. About this time likewise, he obtained the privilege of reading Reynolds's *Discourses*, the first book he had seen on the subject of painting. This again marks the seclusion to which a young man may be confined, although within the precincts of a dense and enlightened population.

His success in the mode of painting now adopted by him was so great that at the age of twenty he found sufficient employment as a portrait painter at low prices to abandon the painting of carriages, just as he had mastered that mystery by his own efforts. He was likewise induced to marry, while yet he had to obtain a profession or property to support a family.

Stuart, as we have seen, took up his residence in Boston in 1805, and his name had previously reached Frothingham; but although desiring above all things to see the great painter, and obtain his instruction, it was far from his thought that such good was obtainable. He had found that coach painters had secrets, which only could be obtained by a long service as an apprentice, and he concluded that a great portrait painter would require still longer servitude or payment of money far beyond his means, before communication of his higher mysteries. At length, after Stuart had moved to Roxbury, and was surrounded by his family, after much debate, the young man determined to approach the awful presence of the first portrait painter in the country.

There was at this time an ingenious painter of signs and ornaments in Boston of the name of Penniman. This man had talents which had attracted the notice of Stuart. Penniman accidentally saw the portrait of a Mr. Foster, painted by Frothingham, and advised him to see Mr. Stuart. The young man with great trepidation walked to Roxbury, determined to gain admission within the Lion's Den. He thought he would present himself as one wanting his picture painted, and make inquiry respecting Mr. Stuart's prices. He was admitted without difficulty, but Stuart was not at home. His son, Charles, received him, answered his questions, and showed him the work of his father.

Encouraged by Penniman, he soon after determined to show one of his own heads to Stuart, and again walked from Charlestown through Boston and over the neck to Roxbury; this time carrying the portrait of Foster. He knocked and Mrs. Stuart opened the door. He presented himself without showing in the first instance that he had brought a picture — leaving it out of sight of whoever might come to the door. 'Your name, sir, and I will announce you.' This appeared as an awful ceremony to the young painter — but he must go on. He gave his name, and was ushered into the old gentleman's painting room. He mustered courage to communicate his business.

'I will tell you anything I know. Have you brought any specimen of your present skill?'

'I have brought a portrait, sir. It is out-of-doors.'

'Bring it in, sir. We don't turn pictures out-of-doors here. Bring it in.'

On the painter's easel was a portrait of Judge Jones, thought by Mr. Frothingham one of his best. Stuart placed the young man's work by the side of it. He asked him what his present business was.

'Coach painting, sir.'

'Stick to it. You had better be a tea-waterman's horse in New York than a portrait painter elsewhere.'

Notwithstanding this damper, Frothingham saw and heard enough to encourage him; and he obtained permission to come again. On his next visit he did not see the painter, who was engaged with a sitter, but his son Charles told him that his father had said, 'That young man's coloring reminds one of Titian's.' This was fixing Frothingham in the pursuit fated for him. From this time forward he carried his portraits to Roxbury, and never went without receiving a lesson of importance. The sixth picture he carried for criticism, he was amply repaid for his long and fatiguing walk by the remark, after due examination, 'You do not know how well you have done this.'

In the year 1810, Stuart said to his pupil — for such Frothingham must now be called — after looking at a recently painted portrait, 'There is no man in Boston, but myself, can paint so good a head,' and not long after, he went further by saying, 'Except myself, there is no man in the United States can paint a better head than that,' pointing to the last his pupil had brought to him.

Mr. Frothingham removed from Charlestown to Salem — it was there I first saw him. He was fully employed, but I remember nothing in his rooms at that time that would justify the high eulogium above given, or that could compare with portraits from his pencil since painted in New York. He was induced to remove to Boston, but Chester Harding had gained the public favor, and even Stuart was left unemployed!

In 1826 Mr. Frothingham removed to New York, where he remains painting heads with great truth, freedom, and excellence, but not with that undeviating employment which popular painters of far inferior talents at the same time find. He has, as he says, been made to remember Stuart's first characteristic advice and remark: 'Stick to coach painting. You had better be a tea-waterman's horse in New York than a portrait painter elsewhere.'

> But this is not a fair estimate of the profession. It will be found by every candid examiner of the disappointments and vexations attending upon the portrait painter that, like all other troubles which befall man, much is owing to himself. It is hard to bear the supercilious conduct of the rich and ignorant who assume the patronizing tone. But it is best to smile in the confidence of superior knowledge. It is hard to have appointments broken which have caused hours of preparation; but it is best to receive a sitter so as to give token of the injury done you, but without ill-humor. When a well-informed person engages a portrait, the engagement is held sacred, but with the vulgar a contract of that nature is not thought binding, although one for a hogshead of tobacco or pipe of rum would be considered as not to be violated. The painter is injured in his feelings through the preparations he makes, and the reliance he places on the faithless individual. But he has no redress, and had better smile than scold. I have heard of painters, who if a sitter came a few minutes beyond the time appointed, would turn him or her away. This is churlish and injures his practice.

It was a great satisfaction to Frothingham that Gilbert Stuart finally took him on as his pupil. It had an electrifying effect upon him, and he became so prominent as a portrait painter that he was elected a member of the National Academy of Design in 1831. The greatest number of his portraits were painted in Boston and Salem, Massachusetts, and New York City. He died in Brooklyn in 1864.

Referring to his intercourse with Gilbert Stuart, another authority makes the following statement: 'His copies of Stuart's portrait of Washington were of very high grade, and his own original portraits have much in them to suggest the painting of his master in color and composition. A number of his portraits are owned by the City of New York, and hang in the old Court House.' (Fielding, *Dictionary of American Painters, Sculptors, and Engravers.*)

A portrait of his of Ann (Francis-Grant) Hall (page 265) which hangs in the picture gallery at Harvard, Massachusetts, is that of a most charming old lady with a benevolent face and smiling blue eyes. She wears a lovely cap of the softest muslin tied under her chin. Her dress is black and her hands rest in her lap. One sees in it at a glance the hand of a master painter. Ann Francis-Grant Hall, born in 1773 and died in 1857, was the second wife of Edward Grant. The portrait came from the Peter C. Brooks Estate at Medford, Massachusetts.

CHAPTER X

Aɴᴅ now we come to one of the most remarkable examples of starting at the foot of the ladder and climbing to
the top, from Primitives to Fame. If anyone thinks he can
reach the top without working to get there, let him read of
the experiences of Francis Alexander, James Frothingham, and,
best of all — Chester Harding. These men began painting
without any instruction whatsoever, and whatever came to
them of good came as a result of their own singleness of purpose, of their untiring efforts that formed a background to the
great talent for painting that they possessed. That methods
of painting change as generations pass does not detract from
their success. In their day they reached so high a standard
in American art that they received the plaudits not only of the
public but of the best of the art critics of their time. What
more can anyone ask for?

An account of Alexander and Frothingham appears in the
previous chapter. Now we turn to Chester Harding, who
leads this little group and is therefore chosen to end the book.
His career was a remarkable one, like a fairytale.

On September 1, 1938, I received a letter from Worthington,
Massachusetts. It read this way:

'My dear Miss Sears:
  'Perhaps you would be interested in the work of a distant
relative of mine, Chester Harding, who lived in the early
1800's and was a portrait painter. There is a book written
by his daughter in 1890. The book tells of his early life when

he first began painting and travelled from town to town making portraits.

'If you think that any information about him would be of service to you I will gladly send it.'

This lady helped me a great deal in regard to Chester Harding. Here is a description of him, which I think will be found interesting.

The generation to which Chester Harding belonged has passed off the stage. He was an old man of commanding figure later in life, with white hair and flowing beard, whose uncommonly tall figure, though slightly bowed by age, was still enough above the average height to make him conspicuous in any assembly; and whose handsome face expressed kindliness and humor. Nature was bountiful to him in an unusual degree, and to uncommon personal attractions added a mind of more than ordinary power, quick perceptions, and a love for the beautiful in nature and art. He was so ready to see and assimilate into his own being all the refinements of cultivated men and manners that to those who saw him for the first time it was difficult to believe that he was actually without school education, and that he had grown to maturity in the wilds of what was then the far West.

His appearance in Boston at that time was greeted with enthusiasm, and for the moment he was the paramount object of interest. . . . He was an incessant worker. The needs of his large family gave him but small opportunity for leisure. He so deeply felt the deficiencies of his own mental training that he was eager to give his children all the educational advantages that money could procure, and they were sent to the best schools of the period. To secure funds to meet these expenses required constant care and forethought, and obliged him to go from city to city to find the supply of sitters which too long a stay in one place was sure to exhaust. This made his life a roving one, and kept him much from home. He was singularly fortunate, however, in his wife. Her uncommon powers of judgment and her thoroughly well-balanced nature made her an admirable counterpoise to his more impulsive temperament. Towards the close of her life, she wrote: 'Tomorrow I shall have been married twenty-four years, and my husband has not been at home for more than ten years of that time. The longest stay he has ever made without going away at all is one year.'

It is safe to say that there are few of the eminent men of the United States who lived through the first thirty years of Mr. Harding's career whom he did not put on canvas. His likenesses, especially of men, were true and lifelike. Among the testimonials which the fidelity of his likenesses were constantly receiving, none pleased Mr. Harding so much as the following. A lady recently died, and her pet cat had been wandering dejectedly around the house, evidently in search of something she missed. At last she entered the room where a likeness (by Harding) of her late mistress was standing on a sofa. The creature at once gave a bound and tried to settle herself in her accustomed place on the lady's lap.

Here is another comment on Chester Harding's personal appearance:

Mr. Harding's personal appearance was very striking. A friend said of him, 'He was the finest specimen of manly beauty I ever saw.' In stature he was far above the average, measuring six feet three in his stockings. His muscular power was prodigious, and one of his brothers relates that when he was eighteen years old his feats of strength were the wonder of the neighborhood. His hands and feet were so large that he was obliged to import his gloves and to have his lasts made for him. The width between his eyes was such that an ordinary pair of spectacles would but half cover them. During the latter part of his life he wore a full beard which, as well as his hair, was almost white, giving him a patriarchal appearance. A few months before his death, he sat to an artist as a model for the head of Saint Peter. He had a quick impulsive nature and after once coming to a decision was very eager to carry out his plans. His wife was fond of giving an account of their wedding as an illustration of this trait.

The wedding had been fixed for February 15, 1815, and on the preceding day the bride was making her last preparations for the great event. The guests had been invited; the wedding cake was in the oven; and her brother had been dispatched to the neighboring town for the white kid gloves and sash.

Presently the bridegroom elect drove up to the door in a sleigh, and after the first salutations had passed announced that he had come to be married on that day, for the snow was melting so fast if they waited twenty-four hours they could not get back to Caledonia, so they were the day beforehand, and his wife was accustomed to say, 'It has been the day beforehand ever since!'

Chester Harding was born in Conway, Massachusetts, in 1792. His parents were poor, and he was brought up like other poor children. His father had moved the family to Deerfield and did farming there. From his own account of himself, Chester Harding says, 'At the age of twelve I was hired out at six dollars a month to a Mr. Graves in Hatfield.' He stayed with him apparently for two years, and at the age of fourteen they moved to the western part of New York State, into Madison County, then an unbroken wilderness. He worked at cutting timber for five years.

Now, about this time war was declared between the United States and Great Britain. Harding went to war as a drummer, but he was taken ill with a prevailing disease that went through the ranks, and was discharged as his time of service was nearly up.

He married Caroline Woodruff, 'a lovely girl of twenty with handsome dark eyes, fine brunette complexion, of an amiable disposition.' He writes of her, 'I fell in love with her at first sight.' He gives an account of their sufferings owing to a lack of funds that is really pitiful. In one of the towns where they went in search of work, he got a chance to paint a sign for a Mr. W. H. Witherell, and this received so much praise that he became a sign painter and followed that trade for a year. About this time he fell in with a portrait painter by the name of Nelson — one of a primitive sort. In watching him work, he first conceived the idea of trying his hand at painting heads.

> I got him to paint me and my wife [he writes] and thought the pictures perfection, and wondered how it was possible for a man to produce such wonders of art. At length my admiration began to yield to an ambition to do the same thing. I thought of it by day and dreamed of it by night, until I was stimulated to make an attempt at painting myself. I got a board, with such colors as I had use of in my trade, and began a portrait of my wife. I made a thing that looked like her. The moment I saw the likeness, I became frantic with delight; it was like the discovery of a new sense. I could think of nothing else. From that time sign painting became odious.

He then tried his hand at painting the portrait of an Englishman who was a travelling baker, for which he received five dollars, and he sent it at once to the latter's mother in London. He also painted portraits of a man and his wife with whom he was boarding, for the amount of twelve dollars each. 'I shall always remember,' he writes, 'the friendship of an apothecary who at this period of my history encouraged me in my attempts at portrait painting, and allowed me to buy any material I needed on credit from his paint and drug store. I had been painting a second portrait of my wife, and asked Nelson, the painter, to come and see it. He declared it to be no more like my wife than like him, and said further it was utter nonsense for me to try to paint portraits at my time of life, for he had been ten years learning the trade.' However, a friend of his who was a doctor came into the room when Nelson had left, and he thought the painting fine and said it was envy that made Nelson condemn the work. So Harding took heart again.

He then gives an account of how this portrait painting took such a hold on him that he neglected his sign painting. The result was that they became terribly short of funds.

> I resorted to every means to eke out a living [he writes]. I have sometimes played the clarionet for a tight-rope dancer, and on market days would play at the window of the Museum to attract a crowd to the exhibition. For each of these performances I would get a dollar. I was strictly temperate in my habits, and seldom spent a sixpence for anything we did not actually need. My brother Horace, the chair maker, was established in Paris, Kentucky. He wrote me he was painting portraits, and that there was a painter in Lexington who was receiving fifty dollars a head. This price seemed fabulous to me. I began to think seriously of trying my fortune in Kentucky. I soon settled upon the idea and acted at once.

It was at this point that his career began as a professional artist. He took a room and painted the portrait of a very popular young man and made a decided hit. He goes on to describe what happened. 'In six months from that time I had painted nearly one hundred portraits at twenty-five dollars a head. The first twenty-five I took rather disturbed the equanimity of my conscience. It did not seem to me that the portraits were intrinsically worth that money. Now I know they were not.'

He had a rather difficult experience in Paris, Kentucky, and tells about it.

> During my stay in Paris [he writes] I was constantly thrown into the society of those who drank. It was the almost universal custom to take a julep before breakfast, and by degrees I fell into the habit of taking my julep and sometimes two. I soon guessed where this would end, for I found I felt uncomfortable unless I had my morning dram. I stopped short at once, and for five years never tasted a drop of ardent spirits. I was sometimes obliged to sip at a glass of wine at the dinner table.

Then he goes on to say:

> Here it was that I mingled for the first time with the tip top of society. I went to the first-class hotels. I found unspeakable embarrassment at the table with so many fine young gentlemen,

PORTRAIT OF DOCTOR HENRY KITTREDGE OF TEWKSBURY,
MASSACHUSETTS
Painted by William Sanford Mason in 1838.
(Description, page 208)

[253]

PORTRAIT OF MRS. HENRY KITTREDGE (NAOMI PINKERTON-
BROWN) OF TEWKSBURY, MASSACHUSETTS
Painted by William Sanford Mason in 1838.
(Description, page 208)

[254]

PORTRAIT OF SARAH ELIZABETH HERSEY ASHTON CALLENDER
(BORN 1816, DIED 1849)
Painted by Joseph Greenleaf Cole in 1840.
(Description, page 211)

[255]

PORTRAIT OF JOHN BELCHER CALLENDER OF BOSTON,
MASSACHUSETTS

Painted by Albert Gallatin Hoit in 1842.

(Description, pages 209, 210)

PORTRAIT OF MARY HERSEY CALLENDER OF BOSTON,
MASSACHUSETTS

Painted by Joseph Greenleaf Cole in 1845.
(Description, pages 210, 211)

PORTRAIT OF BENJAMIN CALLENDER OF BOSTON, MASSACHUSETTS
Artist unknown. Painted about 1850.
(Description, page 211)

PORTRAIT OF THE SECOND WIFE OF BENJAMIN CALLENDER
Artist unknown. Painted about 1850.
(Description, page 211)

PORTRAIT OF GEORGE REED DILL OF WELLFLEET,
MASSACHUSETTS, GRANDFATHER OF MRS. JAMES ERNEST KNOX
OF WELLESLEY, MASSACHUSETTS
Painted by Joseph Greenleaf Cole.
(Description, page 209)

PORTRAIT OF ANNA (PHILLIPS) SHAW
Artist unknown. Painted about 1792.
(Description, page 212.)

PORTRAIT OF A LADY, FROM AN OLD BEACON HILL HOUSE,
BOSTON, MASSACHUSETTS

Painted by Cephas Giovanni Thompson about 1850.

(Description, page 213)

[262]

PORTRAIT OF FRANCIS AMORY OF BOSTON, MASSACHUSETTS
Painted by Ethan Allen Greenwood in 1813.
(Description, pages 207, 208)

PORTRAIT OF MRS. FRANCIS AMORY OF BOSTON, MASSACHUSETTS
Painted by Ethan Allen Greenwood in 1813.
(Description, pages 207, 208)

PORTRAIT OF MRS. ANN FRANCIS-GRANT HALL (BORN 1773, DIED 1857), SECOND WIFE OF EDWARD GRANT

Painted by James Frothingham.

(Description, page 246)

PORTRAIT OF MRS. THOMAS GRAY (MARY STURGIS GORHAM)
AND HER SON GORHAM GRAY

Painted by Francis Alexander in 1835.
Presented by Miss Mary Sturgis Gray.
(Description, pages 238, 239)

[266]

PORTRAIT OF MR. THOMAS GRAY OF BOSTON, MASSACHUSETTS
Painted by Chester Harding in 1830.
Presented by Miss Mary Sturgis Gray.
(Description, page 280)

[267]

PORTRAIT OF MRS. C. BAKER OF SALEM, MASSACHUSETTS
Painted by Chester Harding in 1840.
(Description, page 280)

all so elegantly dressed, with ruffled shirts, rings on their white and delicate fingers, and diamond pins in their bosoms. They no doubt thought me very clownish, as I undoubtedly was. I found little respect paid me by them until I began to attract the attention of their masters. I soon became a sort of lion, and grew very popular among these clerks, especially after I was so advanced in the ways of society as to take my morning juleps. Up to this time, I had thought little of the profession, so far as its honors were concerned, for it indeed had never occurred to me that it was more honorable or profitable than sign painting. Now I began to entertain more elevated ideas of the art, and to desire some means of improvement. Finding myself in funds sufficient to visit Philadelphia, I did so, and spent two months in that city devoting my time entirely to drawing in the Academy and in studying the best pictures, practicing at the same time with the brush. I would sometimes feel a good deal discouraged as I looked at the works of older artists.

Then he goes through periods of discouragement. His ambition would rise, and he would work with even greater vigor than before. 'One good effect of my visit to Philadelphia,' he writes, 'was to open my eyes to the merits of other artists, though it took away much of my self-satisfaction.'

The next place he went to was Cincinnati, where he had the good fortune to make a hit with the first portrait he painted there, which led to many others. Then he went to St. Louis, where he met with an equal success. Now he writes:

My ambition in my profession began to take a higher flight, and I determined to go to Europe. I had accumulated over a thousand dollars in cash, and had bought a carriage and a pair of horses. With these I started with my family for Weston, New York, where my parents were still living, by whom we were warmly welcomed. My success in painting, and especially the amount of money I had saved, was the wonder of the whole neighborhood.

But his grandfather thought it was very little better than

swindling for him to charge forty dollars for one of those effigies, and beseeched him to give up painting and settle down on the farm and, as he expressed it, 'become a respectable man.'

But Chester Harding did not agree to this; his mind was made up on Europe, and he decided to leave his wife and children to his parents and turn his face in that direction. But just as his trunks were packed to go, his mother implored him not to, but told him to settle down on a farm. It ended in his giving in to her wishes, and in buying one hundred and fifty acres of land. He got a carpenter to undertake the building of a house on it, and then started for Washington. His success was so great there that after six months of painting innumerable portraits he returned, and was able in the spring to pay for the new house, and make another payment on the farm, but he was off again almost immediately. Everywhere he went he had all the sitters he could take care of.

While in Northampton [he wrote] I painted the portraits of two gentlemen from Boston. They encouraged me to establish myself in that city. I did so, and for six months rode triumphantly on the top wave of fortune. I took a large room, arranged my pictures, and fixed upon one o'clock as my hour for exhibition. As soon as the clock struck, my bell would begin to ring and people would flock in, sometimes to the number of fifty. New orders were constantly given me for pictures. I was obliged to resort to a book for registering the names of the numerous applicants. As a vacancy occurred, I had only to notify the next on the list and it was filled. I do not think any artist in this country ever enjoyed more popularity than I did — but popularity is often easily won, and as easily lost. Mr. Stuart, the greatest portrait painter this country ever produced, was at this time in his manhood's strength as a painter, yet he was idle half the winter. He would ask of his friends, 'How rages the Harding fever?'

Springfield is a city where he painted some very fine

portraits, and where he made a most delightful impression on those fortunate enough to secure time for sittings. In a letter from Samuel Orne, Esq. to his brother-in-law, Honorable D. A. White of Salem, Massachusetts, he says he feels more and more interest in Mr. Harding the more he sees him. 'In addition to his wonderful genius and his good sense,' he writes, 'he has a frank, generous, open-hearted, unaffected manner which at once secures a stronghold on your best feelings.'

But now the dream of Harding's ambition was to be realized. In August, 1824, he set sail for England, leaving his family with his parents. An account of him came out in *Blackwood's Magazine* shortly after his arrival. In it the author of the article enlarges on the wonders of the man who only about six years ago was occupied in drumming for a militia company, in fitting axe-helves to axes, and was engaged in a number of humble and minor occupations, never having seen a decent picture in his life, and who finally took to sign painting as a means of livelihood, as his pockets were practically empty and he had a family to feed, and from there starting on a career of portrait painting without training, and with no one to back him.

'Mr. Harding,' it goes on to say, 'is now in London; has painted some remarkably good portraits — including one or two of H.R.H. the Duke of Sussex, the head of which is Capital — one of Mr. Owen of Lanark — a portrait of an extraordinary plainness, power, and sobriety; and some others which were shown at Somerset House and Suffolk House.'

Harding tells of starting the portrait of the Duke of Sussex.

January 14th, 1824. Began the portrait of His Royal Highness, the Duke of Sussex. This was the first time I ever had the honor of seeing one of the Royal Family; and of course my approach to this august personage was marked by some little palpitations of the heart; but his affable manners placed me entirely at my ease. In the course of the sitting His Royal Highness spoke warmly of America, and said that he felt a pleasure in being painted by an American artist. In this country it is looked upon as a mark of great distinction to be allowed to paint one of the Royal Family. The Duke is a prodigiously fat man, above six feet high, of very uncommon features, but not intellectual. . . .

Monday, January 19th. Finished the portrait of the Duke. He seems well pleased with it, and seems to take considerable interest in my success. All who have seen the portrait think it the best that was ever taken of His Royal Highness. His Highness gave me a ticket to the Highland's Society Dinner, an annual jubilee from time immemorial. Some two hundred of the highland chiefs and lairds, all in their appropriate costumes, were assembled. It was the grandest affair I ever had the pleasure of witnessing. Every man wore the plaid of his clan. There were five or six of us in black. We were placed at the foot of one of the long tables and had a fine view of the company. Old and young were splendidly dressed, and a gorgeous sight it was. After the regular toasts, such as 'The King,' 'The Royal Family,' 'The Ministers,' and so on, volunteer toasts were given. The Duke of Sussex was the President, and was addressed as the Earle of Inverness, the clans considering that title higher than his English one; . . . Presently I saw the Duke's servant coming down to our end of the table, and approaching me he said, 'His Royal Highness will take wine with you.' I rose, and His Royal Highness half-rose and bowed. Such a mark of distinction was felt by my black-coated neighbors. I found them sociable, and very respectful after that. As soon as the dinner was dispatched the bagpipes were introduced, and the first note started the company to their feet, and nearly the whole assembly joined in the Highland Fling. . . . It was an exciting scene, and continued until the late hour. Some were 'fu' and all were 'unco happy.' As the Duke retired, he honored me with the shake of his hand.

In one of his letters home he gives a delightful account of a spring day in London. He says:

This is a lovely season. All the gaiety of the kingdom is now in full bloom; the park and the gardens are green and inviting.

It is one of the most delightful walks in the world to go to Hyde Park and Kensington Gardens at this time of year. It is the fashion here to go to the Park every day at five or six o'clock and make as great a show as possible. Those who keep carriages never fail of displaying them, and those who do not figure as pedestrians only. It is about a mile from one side of the Park to the other, I mean the Park which is most frequented ... there are from one to two thousand elegant carriages at the same time in the fashionable procession in fine weather, and from fifty to one hundred thousand people of all countries, ages, sexes, and colors promenading the foot walks or sauntering across the green.

But upon retiring from this show to my own room and to serious reflections, I am always struck with the folly of this gay rabble, and it never fails to create a longing for home, and those happy scenes in domestic life, which the world of fashion are strangers to.

I do not doubt if I were to remain here I could establish a permanent character as a painter, and here, of all places in the world, is the artist paid best for his labors. But if I could in five years rise to be President of the British Academy with a 'Sir' tacked upon my name, I would not forego the pleasure of living in America.

A few days later he writes this in his diary:

Saturday, June 27th. Yet in doubt whether it is my duty to stay another year in this country, or to go home to my family and friends. These and like thoughts are constantly haunting my mind. But then I have made the choice of a profession in which I am most anxious and determined to excel. The charm of distinction is dazzling my eyes continually. I have already excited a warm interest with many friends in my behalf, to fail therefore would be painful beyond description. To return to Boston and receive a cold welcome where I have been so warmly patronized would be a sore wound to my pride, and ice to my ambition. Yet it is fair to count upon this to some degree. Public favors and opinions are capricious. There was something novel perhaps in my history that contributed more to my unheard-of success than any merit I possess as a painter. The fact of a man's coming from the backwoods of America, entirely uneducated to paint even a tolerable portrait, was enough to excite some little interest. That source of interest will be cut off on my return. I shall be judged of as one having had all the advantages of the best school of art in Europe; and the probability is that more will be expected of me than is in the power of almost any man to perform. . . .

Saturday, July 31st. Introduced to Irving by Leslie. He is very pleasing in his manners; talks with great volubility, at the same time has a little hesitation or want of fluency in conversation. Called on the Duke of Sussex. He recommends to me to send for my wife and make England my home.

His account of going to see the Duke of Hamilton is quite amusing. He had a letter of introduction to him from the Duke of Sussex.

I took the letter [he writes] and went to the palace with the resolve to see His Grace if possible. After waiting half an hour, the Duke came out from the breakfast table, and very politely asked me into the breakfast room, and invited me to take breakfast, but I declined the honor, and made my business known to him, which was to request the Duke to sit for a picture for the Duke of Sussex. He readily complied and asked me to send for my portmanteau, and take up my residence with him.

I soon commenced the portrait. . . . Five o'clock came, and I began to dress for dinner. Felt some anguish from fear and wished the ordeal of dinner were over. Six o'clock came at last, and I was ushered into the dining-room. In a short time I began to realize that my titled companions were very like other people, and in a short time more my nerves became steady, though I could not entirely refrain from moving my knife and fork a little, or playing with my bread, or in some other way betraying a want of ease. There was a display of great magnificence; servants all in livery — splendid gentlemen followed them. The Duchess made tea with her own fair hand and was, besides, very agreeable. At half-past eleven I set off to bed; and on my way thanked my stars it was all over and matters stood no worse....

I am obliged to own to myself that this style of living is very charming. Everything around one savors strongly of title, wealth, and antiquity. We breakfast at ten, lunch at two, and dine at six. The Duchess is pretty, witty, and sociable. Lord Archibald Hamilton is staying here at this time, and is a very clever man. I think I shall succeed very well. All the household servants have been in to look at the picture and say it could not be more like. As I walk about the grounds the laborers, old and young, lift their hats as I pass them. This respect and reverence sit but ill on me who have been in all the early part of life in as humble a sphere as those who pay it. What freak of fortune is this which has raised me from the hut in my native wilds to the table of the Duke of the realm of Great Britain? By another freak I may be sent back to the hovel again, but [he adds reflectively] not to enjoy those innocent pleasures that were mixed with the toils of boyhood.

While on this visit he made a pilgrimage to Bothwell Castle. It was a beautiful day, and this new experience was going to his head like wine. He sat down upon a rock among the ruins and looked around at the surrounding walls, once a part of a seemingly impregnable fortress. 'I thought of the thousands who had died in their defense,' he wrote. 'The same sun shone on them that now shines on me. They were as full of ambition as I am, and thought as little of this generation as I do of those yet unborn; and where are they now?'

This thought sobered him, and he sat reflecting on this theme until late in the afternoon.

Then came a day when the portrait was finished. He writes of it thus:

Sunday night. After dinner took leave of the family. The Duke urged me to stay a few days longer. The Duchess wished me every success, and Lord Archibald pressed me to call upon him in London. The Duke said if it was at any time in his power to serve me, he should be most happy to do so. He ordered a portrait of His Royal Highness, the Duke of Sussex. He advised me not to think of returning to my own country at present.

Thus ended a visit of ten days that I shall long remember with delight and gratitude, but no honor which a Royal Duke or anyone else in this country can confer upon me will ever make me feel that pleasure which the remembrance of the kindness of the people of Boston have done.

Instead of returning to America, after much thought, he decided to send for his wife and children, and they arrived on the 24th of September, 1825. He then found that it was not at all what he hoped it would be. It was one thing to lionize an unattached man, but quite another to include his family, and he found that invitations still came to him, but his wife had to sit by herself in their rooms. This did not make for happiness for either of them.

They went to Glasgow, and he painted a number of portraits there, but the orders were not coming in as plentifully as before, and he found himself in a very difficult position. He had been living up to the last cent in order to keep to the standard he thought advisable towards presenting a good appearance, and now he was facing the cold fact that he could not possibly afford to continue in this extravagance. He decided to return to America.

One cannot help being somewhat amused at his feelings at being back in Boston after the royal time he had been having, being flattered by dukes and duchesses and staying in their palaces. The morning after his arrival in the city, where he and his family put up at the Exchange Hotel, he walked out to wander through the familiar streets. His diary gives a description of it.

I walked out with the children [he wrote]. Everything had a diminutive appearance. The Common was not what it used to be in old time. The children took but little interest in what they saw, but they had one wonder to tell their mother of, that they had not seen a single beggar....

I met many old friends who gave me a hearty welcome home.

In a letter to S. F. L. he writes:

At Home, No. 9 Cedar Street. You will want to know how much rent I pay. I have taken a house for two years perhaps at four hundred dollars per year with the privilege of vacating it at the expiration of one by paying twenty-five dollars extra. We are within a ston 's throw of the Misses Cabot and very near Mrs. Eliot and Mrs. Minot, all of whom are pleasant neighbors, you know. I am happy to tell you that my professional labors have increased rather than otherwise, and that in spite of the costs of furnishing, I have still a little left to feed upon in case of a 'rainy day.'

He then goes to Canada. On his return he moves to another house, 16 Beacon Street, this time. But he goes to Baltimore in search of work and has good success. On his return he writes as follows:

I now began my career again in Boston; not as I did on my first appearance in that city, for then I was entirely self-taught, and little could be expected of one from the backwoods; but now I come fresh from the schools of Europe, and with some reputation. I felt keenly how much more would be required of me to fill the expectations of the connoisseurs and patrons of art. My first picture was of Emily Marshall, and I know the picture, then the reigning beauty of Boston. No artist's skill could be put to a severer test; for her beauty depended much upon the expression of her animated face, which, when lighted up in conversation, was bewitchingly lovely. I did not succeed to my own satisfaction, but others seemed well pleased.

The following is taken from a letter from Miss E. S. Quincy of Quincy, Massachusetts, to one of Mr. Harding's children:

How well I remember both his studios. The first was in Beacon Street near the Athenaeum. I can see the portraits ranged on the floor, for they succeeded each other so rapidly there was no time to frame and hang them. His second studio was in Cornhill, and I can see the portraits of Emily Marshall and Mrs. Webster (the wife of Daniel Webster) in the dress she wore at Bunker Hill on the day of the celebration, June 17, 1825, a pearl-colored hat and pelisse. It was impossible, as your father says, to catch the living fascination on Emily Marshall's face, but his portrait, I am told, is the only record which remains of her beauty. She was the most celebrated belle who ever appeared in our country, and was as much admired by ladies as by gentlemen, and although she was ever before the public, as it were, her celebrity never waned. If she walked the street I always expected a smile and a bow from her, and never passed her father's house without looking up to see her beautiful face brought out in full relief against the crimson curtain.

Chester Harding has more to tell about his fees for painting portraits. He writes: 'I now charge one hundred dollars for a head. My former price was fifty dollars.'

In the latter part of the summer of 1830, he went with his family to Springfield, and was so pleased with the place that he says, 'I exchanged my house on Beacon Street for one in Springfield, which has been our home ever since.'

In 1845 his wife died on the 27th of August, after an illness of only three days.

In 1846 Mr. Harding made a second trip to England. He wandered about the streets of London.

I find nobody in town that I want to see [he writes]. I have strolled about a good deal, visiting my old haunts. Yesterday, I went to the National Gallery, and looked at the works of the old masters. I find that most of them do not please me as much as they did formerly. I am disappointed in the modern paintings I have seen. I find on looking at my old pictures that I was at least twenty-five years younger in the art than I am now, whatever I may be in years.

From London he goes to Glasgow, and there he is impressed with how old all his former friends look.

> It is impossible to feel [he writes] that these grey-headed men are the same persons that I knew so intimately when I was here before. I have looked into the glass to see if I can discover any change in my own looks, and sometimes I think I can discover a slight one. [*Author's comment:* Fortunate man not to discover more than that!]

It is interesting to note Mr. Harding's estimate of Daniel Webster, whom he knew very well, after the hosts of celebrated persons he met in Europe. He writes upon his return:

> I do think him the greatest man I ever came in contact with. He is not only full of wisdom and delightful anecdote, but of that sort of playful wit which startles the more, coming from the same fountain as it does, with the wisest maxims that man ever uttered. With all this eulogism, he is far from being a perfect character. He lacks many of the essentials requisite in the formation of a good man. He lacks sympathy. He has the art of making many admirers, but few friends.

It was during this winter (1847) that he painted the full-length portrait of Mr. Webster which hangs on the wall of the Athenaeum, and also that of Mr. Henry Clay which hangs in the City Hall in Washington.

In 1848 Chester Harding went to Baltimore to hunt up the pay from subscribers who gave him the order to paint Mr. Clay's portrait. It was a most unhappy experience. Many of the subscribers flatly refused to pay up, 'on the ground that by his letter he has blasted his prospects for his nomination and election.'

Full of anxiety and annoyance over this state of things, he writes, 'I like the climate of the North, I like the people of the North, I like my home in the North, and I mean to go North very soon.'

Although Mr. Harding continued to follow his profession during the winter months, even to the last year of his life, his active career as an artist began to decline from this time. He spent his winters in some of the large cities as Boston, New

York, Washington, St. Louis, but though familiar with them all, none seemed to be so much like home, or claimed so large a share of his affection, as Boston. He writes of this:

> I have been from infancy such a cosmopolite that I can hardly claim any portion of the United States as home; yet I feel that I owe more to Boston than any other place. More of my professional life has been spent in that city than anywhere, and it is around it that my most grateful recollections cluster. The liberal patronage that I have received and the friendships I have formed there make the place dear to me.... The most liberal patronage I have enjoyed, has been perhaps from the Lawrences. I have painted all of them, and many of their children. My full-length portrait of Amos Lawrence I consider the best thing I ever did in my whole artistic career. I also painted a full-length of Abbott Lawrence.

There are two portraits by Chester Harding in the collection at Harvard, one of which (page 267) is that of Mr. Thomas Gray, son of Thomas and Ruth (Davis) Gray, born in Yarmouth, Massachusetts, July 4, 1798. Mr. Gray wears a black velvet coat with fancy gilt buttons on it. The collar is white and the stock that binds around it is also white. He has brown hair and the flesh tints of his face are beautifully modelled. It is the work of a master painter. The background of this portrait is a sort of grey blue, a color which Chester Harding was very fond of using in his backgrounds, and is identical with that of the other portrait by him of Mrs. C. Baker of Salem, Massachusetts, which is in the collection. (Page 268.) She is a true type of the old Salem aristocracy, and looks very much like the Lee family. She has a lovely florid smiling face, and sits up very straight. Her hair is beautifully done, being parted in the middle and drawn to each side of her face, and on it she wears an embroidered muslin cap, the crisp tabs of which fall down as far as her waist. She wears a black satin dress with a muslin collar edged with an embroidered ruffle. It is an inspiration to look at these two portraits and think of the long road Harding had to travel over before he came to the hilltop from which he emerged into the life of an artist of fame.

The latter years of Mr. Harding's life were shadowed by the War of the Rebellion. He was the more oppressed by them as he had four sons in the contest, two on each side.

The last portrait he painted was that of General Sherman, and he considered it to be one of his best.

His death was very sudden — such as he had always hoped for. He was feeling in excellent health when he caught cold, and died before any of his family could reach his bedside. He died on April 1, 1866. The newspapers of that period are full of eulogies of him, and give detailed accounts of his life, here and in England, and of the great popularity of his paintings.

He leads in fame the itinerant portrait painters of the period of which this is written.

As has been said, the three outstanding men who emerged from the profession of itinerant artists to that of famous portrait painters on this side of the water at the beginning of the nineteenth century are Chester Harding, Francis Alexander, and James Frothingham. There were others who made lasting names for themselves, but these three lead the list, with Chester Harding to the front.

THE END

APPENDIX

AN ASSISTANCE TO THOSE WHO ARE COLLECTING

APPENDIX

Jeremiah W. Wetherby was born in 1780. His birthplace was Stowe, Massachusetts, and this fact was recorded in Boxboro. I corresponded with the librarian at Boxboro, but she could not give me any facts beyond this.

Isaac Wetherbee flourished as an artist in Boston in 1842, when he exhibited in the Athenaeum Gallery. The Directory of that year gives 'Isaac *A.*'

Winthrop Chandler, youngest son of William and Jemima (Bradbury) Chandler, was born in Woodstock, Connecticut, April 6, 1747. I saw a portrait by him of Nathaniel Chandler in Lancaster, Massachusetts.

Early in life, after the death of his father, he chose portrait painting as a profession, and it is claimed he studied art in Boston. Some of his portraits are preserved in Woodstock and Thompson, Connecticut, and in Worcester and Petersham, Massachusetts. In addition to his portrait painting, he employed his time in house painting, carving, etc. He died July 29, 1790, in Thompson, Connecticut. The *Worcester Spy* of August 19, 1790, contains an obituary notice.

Deacon Robert Peckham, born in Petersham, Massachusetts, in 1785, became an itinerant portrait painter, travelling mostly in the country districts, but established for a while in Boston, Massachusetts. Most of his portraits are rather flat, hard and stiff, but evidently good likenesses. Peckham painted John Greenleaf Whittier in 1833.

There was an itinerant artist by the name of Fletcher, and another by the name of Brewer. The latter made rather a specialty of children, and many of the children in pantalettes are his work. These painters painted especially in New Hampshire and Vermont.

I came across a portrait by G. F. Bancroft of Nancy Peck, painted in 1848. This was a fine portrait, and full of character.

I saw a portrait of Jane Gould, painted by I. A. Wetherbee in 1845. This was of a little girl painted after her decease. Wetherbee made rather a specialty of this kind of painting. I also saw a portrait of Mr. Gould painted by Wetherbee in 1845 in Boston. This was a fine portrait, well painted, and evidently a good likeness.

There was a painter named Thomas Badger, 'who specialized in miniatures, but did oil work as well. He was working in Boston from 1836 till 1859' (Fielding). I saw two portraits of his in Fitchburg, Massachusetts.

There was an itinerant painter by the name of E. Wilson, who was a New Hampshire artist. I saw two portraits of his of Reverend and Mrs. Frank Cooper of Antrim, New Hampshire.

There was an itinerant portrait painter by the name of J. Gilbert, who came from New Bedford, and did a great deal of painting around there.

There was an itinerant portrait painter by the name of Robert Street. I saw a portrait of his which was very good. He was born in 1796 and for a certain number of years was a resident of Philadelphia, where he did much excellent work. He held an exhibition of his portraits in 1840.

I saw two excellent portraits painted by Mrs. Ruth Bascom of Jacob Puffer and Sarah Hawkes Whiting Puffer in 1812.

There was an itinerant painter named Alvan Clark, who was born in Ashfield, Massachusetts, in 1804. He was principally an engraver, and was employed in Boston at one time, where he made water-colors and India-ink portraits. He also painted in oils, and did a good deal of work in Providence, Rhode Island, New York, and Fall River, Massachusetts. At the age of forty he became interested in telescopes and made the first achromatic lenses manufactured in this country. He died in Cambridge, Massachusetts, in 1864.

Among other miniatures which he painted, apart from his oil paintings, was one of Mr. Lucius M. Sargent of Boston.

At Kennebunk, Maine, there was a very popular itinerant portrait painter named Badger, whose work became widespread.

There was an itinerant portrait painter named Jonathan Mason, Jr., who lived on Mt. Vernon Street, Boston. He exhibited portraits at the Boston Athenaeum in 1828 and 1834, among these being one painted of himself.

There were twin brothers born in Malden, Massachusetts, in 1834, named Cyrus Cobb and Darius Cobb. The former, for about twenty years, was identical with his brother, they both doing the same things. He painted portraits of Doctor A. P. Peabody, Doctor Appleton, and others, but really devoted himself to law, which was his profession. He died in 1905.

Darius Cobb also painted many portraits and some landscapes and figure pieces. He also cut busts in marble. He was a frequent lecturer on art subjects in Boston and elsewhere. He died in 1919.

There was an itinerant artist named F. H. Wilder, who painted around Fitchburg and Leominster, Massachusetts, in 1846.

I came across a portrait of C. G. Beauregard painted about 1840. It was very primitive.

An itinerant artist named P. Reed painted around Leominster about 1840.

I came across two portraits of Fanny and Freddy W. Jones, painted by Charles S. Gibson. These were children's portraits and not especially good.

I came across a fine portrait of Ebenezer Gage of Charlestown, Massachusetts, painted by J. Moron. It was excellent. As I remember it the date was around 1832.

I also came across a portrait of a child in a blue dress with pantalettes, holding a bell in one hand and a letter in the other, painted by E. W. Blake, and another one of a boy wearing a white ruff around his neck, named Charles Holt of North Andover, by the same itinerant artist.

E. Bowers was an itinerant artist who painted around 1858.

There was an itinerant painter named O. I. Bears, who did a great deal of painting around New London in 1835. There was a portrait brought to my notice of a handsome young woman with a child in her arms. It was signed 'O. I. Bears, 1835, New London.' The picture was a very pleasing one.

I came across a portrait of a man by M. B. Tenney, 1840.

There was also an itinerant portrait painter named James Coyle, who painted around Massachusetts.

I saw a painting of a young girl, which was very charming, which was signed by an itinerant painter named Ingalls in 1848, Concord, New Hampshire. He was also a well-known painter of miniatures.

There was an itinerant artist named Willis Seaver Adams, who did a good deal of painting around Springfield, Massachusetts. An account of him can be found in King's *Handbook of Springfield*.

An itinerant artist named Fordham also did a good deal of work around Springfield.

A lady wrote me about a man named Hubbard who was very successful in making silhouettes and also oil portraits. She said she had two of them, one painted in 1818 and the other in 1839. The first was painted in Boston, and the other in New York. She says that Hubbard came to this country with Gilbert Stuart and paid his way about painting silhouettes.

There was a successful portrait painter named Albert Fisher. He was born in Massachusetts in 1792 and died in 1863. In later years he had a studio in Boston and painted many portraits.

Another lady wrote me about her owning portraits of her grandparents and great-grandparents done in 1827 by a portrait painter by the name of Appleton. They were very well done. 'I have nothing to tell,' she said, 'as I was the last of the family, but I imagine he must have been an itinerant painter, and probably painted in and around Otisville, Maine.'

A gentleman wrote me about a man called Charles the Painter. He says: 'We have three group paintings of my grandfather. If he were living now he would be one hundred and forty years old. The portraits were painted in Keene, New Hampshire.'

In Worcester, Massachusetts, there was an itinerant painter named Charles Curtis who painted oil portraits and miniatures. An advertisement of his appeared in the Worcester newspaper. It runs thus:

Charles Curtis

respectfully gives notice to the ladies and gentlemen of Worcester and its vicinity that he should be happy to serve them in the line of his profession.

Correct likenesses taken, either in portrait or miniature sizes, at prices from three to thirty dollars. Specimens of his work may be seen at his room in this building occupied by Mr. Theophilus B. Weston, opposite the jail.

Worcester, August 4, 1824.

This was found pasted inside an old trunk.

I received another letter that had this enclosure: 'My mother's and father's portraits were painted by Mr. Fordham at Springfield, Massachusetts.'

The following was written to me in a letter dated September 27, 1938: 'We have in our family a small portrait of my grandmother, painted on shell, or something similar. She was born in 1818, and the picture was painted in 1836 by Fuller of Deerfield. My grandmother lived in Orange, or New Salem, Massachusetts.' Fuller of Deerfield was the artist, George Fuller. He was born in Deerfield in 1822, therefore the portrait 'on shell, or something similar' must have been painted when he was a boy of fourteen.

I received a letter from a lady: 'My children's great-great-grandfather on their father's side was George Gasner, an itinerant artist. He was born in Germany in 1811, and came to this country in his youth and died in 1861 in Chicopee Falls, Massachusetts. He painted portraits and miniatures. I understand that in the Springfield Public Library in the Hampton County Book is an article on George Gasner, the artist. I have several family portraits and a miniature by George Gasner.' This was dated from Putnam, Connecticut.

I received a letter from Manchester, Connecticut, about an itinerant portrait painter named Charles Grinniss. 'My aunt, who is eighty-six years old and very alert and has lived in this section of

Buckingham since she was sixteen years old, told me this itinerant artist's name.'

Another letter I received gave this bit of information: Marvin S. Robbins, who lived in Middlefield and Becket, 1813–1872, painted portraits in several Middlefield homes, as well as many others.

A letter from Hyannis, Massachusetts, gives the following information: 'My great-grandfather, Arnold Steere of Woonsocket, Rhode Island, supported his family by portrait painting, travelling from Woonsocket as far as Philadelphia, dates 1815–1832. He was a very fine portrait painter. We are in possession of his self-painted and family portraits in oil 110 years old.'

In another letter the same correspondent says: 'Arnold Steere was born in Smithfield, Rhode Island (now Woonsocket), in 1792. He became a member of the National Academy of Arts and Sciences of New York and Philadelphia, and was a fellow member with Samuel Morse, the artist.' Arnold Steere died rather young in 1832. He earned his living as an artist.

This comes from another correspondent, about the artist, John Tolman. (Dunlap speaks of him in volume III of his book.) '1690, my father was well acquainted with John Tolman. (He called him Jack Tolman.) I often heard my father speak of him in Boston about eighty years ago. I learned from what he said that Tolman was an itinerant portrait painter, and self-taught artist. He travelled all over the country, practicing his profession. At one time he was stopping at a hotel in New Orleans, and the building totally collapsed while he was sleeping. This, according to his story, was almost equal to assisting at an earthquake.'

The following is about the itinerant artist Alfred J. Wiggin. A lady writing me about him says that she has in her possession portraits of her father and mother painted between 1847 and 1853 by that artist. 'I have before me,' she writes, 'his receipted bill of 1853 that runs thus: "Painting portrait Ten Dollars." Many people in this town of Pigeon Cove had portraits by Wiggin.'

Here is a quotation from a letter dated Wolfboro, New Hampshire: 'Willard, who painted the "Spirit of 1776," worked as a painter of scenes on carriages in a shop in Wellington, Ohio, in his youth, and also painted portraits.'

A lady wrote me about two paintings she had seen by E. W. Blake, an itinerant portrait painter. The technique, she said, was very much like that of William Prior.

Some time ago I came across a portrait painted by Brewster, of twin boys, and one also by J. H. Grout, likewise an itinerant portrait painter.

A letter from Leominster gave me the following record of an itinerant portrait painter, who signed his name 'N. Brooks.' He painted the portraits of the writer's grandparents. His real name was Newton Brooks. He was born in New Ipswich, New Hampshire.

Here is a quotation from a letter I received from Middleton, Massachusetts. 'I have a painting by Asa Bushby of my great uncle, painted about one hundred years ago. This artist did most of his work in and around Danvers, Massachusetts. His home was in what is now called Peabody.'

There was an itinerant portrait painter named Bald Hughes. He painted a number of portraits in Boston and vicinity.

I came across a portrait of Wendell Phillips signed by the artist G. W. Newell.

I saw a portrait of Martha Anthony of Malden, Massachusetts, painted by Alvan Clark, who was painting around Boston in 1836. This artist was born in Ashfield, Massachusetts, in 1804, and was quite successful.

I came across two very crude portraits by an artist named N. B. Onthank of Francis Adams and his wife, painted in 1848. Onthank was not a New England man. He came from New York State, but wandered into Massachusetts plying his art.

BIBLIOGRAPHY

SOME sources from which I have gathered information are:

Arnold, *Art and Artists in Rhode Island.*

Benjamin, S. G. W. *Art in America.*

Bolton, Charles K. *Workers with Line and Color in New England.* (Unpublished manuscript.)

Clement, Clara Erskine, and Laurence Hutton. *Artists of the Nineteenth Century and Their Works.*

Dresser, Louisa. *Seventeenth-Century Painting in New England.*

Dunlap, William. *The History of the Arts of Design in the United States.*

Fielding, Mantle. *Dictionary of American Painters, Sculptors, and Engravers.*

Foote, Henry Wilder. *Catalogue of Portraits in the Essex Institute.*

French, H. W. *Art and Artists in Connecticut.*

Isham, Samuel. *History of American Painting.*

The Metropolitan Museum, New York. *Life in America.*

Morgan, John Hill. *Gilbert Stuart and His Pupils.*

Tuckerman, Henry T. *Book of the Artists.*